# Taking Action

# Taking Action

Creating Social Change through Strength,
Solidarity, Strategy, and Sustainability

Rebecca L. Toporek and Muninder Kaur Ahluwalia

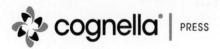 cognella® | PRESS

www.cognella.com          800-200-3908

# Dedication

I have enormous gratitude for my students, colleagues, and mentors as well as the community activists who inspire, model, and instigate opportunities for social action. I am thankful to the lessons of leaders such as Corrina Gould of Save West Berkeley Shellmound and scholars such as Drs. Janet Helms, Patricia Arredondo, Derald Wing Sue, and Don Pope-Davis, to name just a few. Every day, the love, patience, and support from my partner Phil and my children Kaiya and Dylan, keep me grounded and committed to working toward positive change. I thank my parents, Doreen and Walter, for their belief in justice, fairness, and peace and the values they instilled in me. I treasure and feel thankful for the unconditional support and caring of my sisters and brother, Cynthia, Veronica, and Dan. Finally, I am forever grateful for all of the people who stand up in the face of injustice as well as those who face oppression and continue to move forward.

—Rebecca

I am grateful for the blessings and opportunities provided by Waheguru (God), and the Sikh religious teachings, which keep seva (service) and justice at my core. The strength of communities on the margin fueled my passion. My mentor, Lisa Suzuki, taught me how to be a professor who centralizes caring for others. I have learned from my brothers, sisters (in law), nieces, and nephews, who all promote justice in their own ways. My partner, Henry, gifted me endless patience, lifted me up when life got me down, and has taught me to see things in new, extraordinary ways. And my parents, Devinder Kaur and Daljit Singh, provided the foundation of everything that is good and just in my life, and taught me to right every wrong—no matter the personal price. Every success I have had is because of them.

—Muninder

# Contents

# Acknowledgments

We would like to thank Dr. Daljit Singh Ahluwalia, Veronica Cox, Dr. Tyce Nadrich, Carlos Flores, Bryan O. Rojas Araúz, and Dr. Jacqueline V. Reza for their time and thoughtful feedback on initial drafts of this workbook.

# section 1

**Opening and Centering**

# chapter one

# Getting Started

Injustice is present in every aspect of our lives. Daily, even hourly, there are updates and calls for action: health care, net neutrality, immigration, employment, poverty, environment, and more. This constant stream of information and alarms can be overwhelming if you want to make a difference, especially because it often comes with little or no guidance on how to navigate it all. For some of us, we have a clear path and know where our efforts are best used. For others of us, we want to respond but become overwhelmed and don't act on any of them. Social media feeds (e.g., Facebook, Twitter, Instagram, Snapchat) are loaded with calls to action and actively engaged users. Yet, whether our online activism is translated to actual action is questionable. Daisy Prado, communications strategist, stated it well (2017):

> I'm not saying that everyone needed to fly out to Washington D.C. for the Women's March or that everyone can afford to spend time volunteering on the weekends, but it's not enough to just post a selfie and say that you are a feminist. What are you *actually* doing to help advance women's rights? Are you donating to Planned Parenthood? Are you volunteering to mentor young girls? Are you opening doors for women in your workplace? (https://www.huffington-post.com/entry/how-woke-twitter-can-be-problematic_us_5910c559e4b0f71180724740)

We like this quote because it speaks to the power of taking action in multiple ways with a commitment to long-term change. This also resonates with the idea that it is important to know what a movement is about, where you fit, what you can contribute, who is affected, and how you can support their efforts. Fighting against most injustices will take a long time and take many actions by many people to make a difference.

## Who Are We?

We (Rebecca and Muninder) met in 2000 during our predoctoral internship at University of California–Berkeley Counseling and Psychological Services. We each came to this work with experience and motivation to address oppression in our personal and professional lives. We bonded around our commitment to be more multiculturally competent in counseling and in our work in the community. We saw how people's experiences were often shaped by what was happening in their lives, in the community, even at national and international levels, and we wanted to do something about it. In this book, we will speak directly to you, the reader, and ask you to share your inner thoughts, feelings, and behaviors, so we thought it might be helpful to share a little about ourselves. In the next few paragraphs, we will introduce each other as our first activity.

Muninder Ahluwalia (left) and Rebecca Toporek (right)

## Rebecca

Rebecca is a mother, daughter, counselor, psychologist, professor, friend, Zumba aficionado, aspiring *bachatera*, and a member of multiple communities. She is quite brilliant, hardworking, and extraordinary in all her roles. She is a natural caretaker of others, and I (Muninder) am often reminding her to take care of herself. When Rebecca and I first met, what I noticed most about her is her kindness and her daily preparedness to be a strong ally for others, even when she has too much on her plate, and even if it may have negative personal or professional consequences for her. I am often struck at her consciousness and commitment to deeply understand people's experiences with marginalization and oppression. She is acutely aware of her privileges as a White, middle-class woman and is always trying to undo oppression. As a White woman, Rebecca has learned from other White women and men, but also from People of Color in her personal and professional life; she is deeply grateful for this learning and for the generosity from her elders who took her under their wings.

Rebecca was raised in a family that kept justice as a core value. Close to her heart and her work are issues of homelessness, racism, and the impact of social and economic inequity in higher education. At the time of the writing of this book, Rebecca is professor and chair of her department, where she is surrounded by many colleagues and students who are justice-oriented advocates. She trains future counselors to work with individuals, families, communities, and systems to promote mental health and wellness. In her work and in her home community, Rebecca helps others work more effectively with people from different backgrounds, advocates for those who need it, and engages in social action. On her days off from work, Rebecca and her family often engage in some community event related to advocacy in the San Francisco Bay Area. She and her husband have raised critically conscious, thoughtful, and generous children whom I love being around.

## Muninder

Muninder is a devoted daughter, sister, and aunt, amazing friend, loving partner, brilliant professor, fierce advocate, and community member. She loves living in New York and being a part of the city salsa communities, educational communities, the Sikh community, and, most of all, her family. I (Rebecca) have learned so much from watching her speak out, over and over again, when she sees injustice, especially in response to societal discrimination, miseducation, and bigotry. Muninder has found ways to use what she has learned personally from her family and faith, and in her profession, to identify and address issues of injustice. Whether she is meeting with community members, talking with media, teaching, or writing, she strives to pay attention to the ways that culture, history, and oppression show up, and then illuminates how things could be different. As a Sikh and Indian woman, Muninder has witnessed the impact of national fears and bias on communities of color, including religious minority communities such as Sikhs and Muslims. This was striking in September 2001 when, shortly after Muninder returned to New York from Berkeley, the World Trade Center was hit as a part of terrorist attacks. The pain and fear felt in the city and country was accompanied by a dramatic increase in hate crimes toward Sikh and Muslim individuals. Later, in 2012, the mass shooting by a White man at a Sikh gurdwara in Oak Creek, Wisconsin, brought more pain and urgency to act, raising awareness and policy change. In her professional life, Muninder is a professor of counseling at a public university in New Jersey mentoring graduate students toward their goals of being school, higher education, addictions, and mental health counselors and counselor educators. She is nationally known for her research and writing in multicultural counseling and experiences of people who are marginalized, especially due to race or religious oppression. I (Rebecca) have learned so much from her and am thankful she has been willing to share in the writing of this book.

Hopefully, this brief introduction gives you a picture of who we are that will be useful as we talk throughout the book. In the chapters that follow, we will alternately share personal examples—not as a template, but rather as illustrations of possible ways to engage with the activities.

## Why Engage in Social Action?

We assume that because you are reading this, you have something you care about. In fact, some of you may already be doing a lot and are looking for reinvigoration or to increase the tools you already have. So, you probably already know that when you truly care about something, you act on it. We demonstrate that we care about something by supporting it, nurturing it, sharing it with others, and sustaining it. For some of us, it goes beyond simply caring; our safety and life (and that of our families and communities) depend on it. In an interview with DeRay McKesson, an activist and former middle school educator, Combat Jack asked, "What shifted in you as an educator … what was the breaking point that really made you respond and react?" DeRay responded,

> In Blackness we are always erasure and erasure manifests in two ways, one is either the story is never told, or it's told by everyone but you. And in this case, we became unerased. Black people got to tell their story in real time … There was this moment of being

out on the street [in St. Louis], I got tear gassed, and I went, "this is not the America that I know." I once believed in America that's not this, but I'm standing in this. Right, and in this moment I commit to fight differently. I think about all the kids that I taught and they deserve something better than this. And I said "I'll do my part." I've had all these incredible experiences and I'm still not free. (https://soundcloud.com/thecombatjackshow/the-deray-mckesson-episode)

For some of us, we feel like it is a choice, and we have a sense of responsibility or want a better future. Taking action can also be good for us. There are numerous studies that demonstrate that giving, volunteering, and engaging in social action for causes and people we care about result in better mental health. Some of the benefits noted are increased sense of empowerment and purpose, relationships and camaraderie, and feeling a greater sense of control. It would be unrealistic for us to ignore that social action, activism, and advocacy can also be stressful, and there is a potential for burnout. It's important to engage in advocacy and activism in ways that can help maintain health, happiness, and positive relationships. It is with this knowledge that we present this workbook.

We each have motivations for engaging in social action as well as challenges and barriers. This workbook was written within and for the context of the United States, and thus some of the political structures and strategies may be unique to this country. While some things are U.S.-focused, the planful approach taken in this workbook can be applied in a global context. We use the term social justice to refer to a condition of fairness and equity in resources as well as conditions and treatment that convey and reflect respect and dignity. Social action is used here to refer to action we take toward addressing injustices and oppression, particularly within systems such as societal, legislative, or organizational practices or policies. Some reflection on your current and potential role in furthering social justice will be helpful as you work through this workbook. Each reader will find some parts more helpful than others. Though we have prepared the workbook with a start and an end, it does not need to be followed in a linear way. There is no right way to use it. Our goal is to provide you with support for the social action you want to engage in and the way *you* want to engage in it.

## Engaging in Social Action

We suggest three aspects to engaging in social action: awareness, information, and behavior. *Awareness* includes recognizing that something unjust is happening, understanding your own reactions to that injustice, and understanding your place in that situation. Recognizing that something

unjust is happening requires paying attention to your surroundings, listening and observing, occasionally looking up from your cell phone, and even
having conversations with the people around you. *Information* involves
understanding the situation as well as knowing about the larger context,
such as the discrimination that occurs in your community. *Behavior* is what
you actually do when you become aware of injustice. In the next chapter,
we will examine this in more depth, but for now, jot down a few thoughts
below to set the stage for thinking about yourself and social action.

### ACTIVITY 1.1

### You and Social Action

Reflect and summarize why it's important to you to take social action, make
your voice heard, and/or advocate for issues or people you care about.

- What motivates you to engage in social action or advocacy for
  this issue?
- What are your challenges in taking action? What makes it difficult or
  seems to hinder you from taking action?

This interactive workbook is designed to help you move forward to
make an impact on the issues you care about. We will first present activities
for identifying a focus for your efforts. Then, we use a four-part approach
to guide you through a strategic process of: 1) identifying your strengths
and resources (Strengths); 2) connecting with others (Solidarity); and 3)
developing effective strategies (Strategies); while 4) taking care of yourself
and the ones you love (Sustainability).

**FIGURE 1.1** S-Quad: Strengths, solidarity, strategies, and sustainability

By including exercises, information, and resources, our goal is to help you become a more active participant in the world around you. Practice makes perfect, so we encourage you to complete the activities and, where possible, implement them. We understand that each person has their own style, preferences, and life demands. Work at your own pace to best suit your style and the things you care about. One thing is certain: we are all different in what we do well, what motivates us, what feels fulfilling, and what keeps us going. A common thread is that being engaged not only helps society, but it is good for our health as well. Fortunately, social change needs all kinds of people and all kinds of strategies. Any one of us can make a difference.

# Gaining Focus

## What do you care about?

Naomi Klein, in her TED Talk about how "shocking events can spark positive change," talks about current large-scale crises (e.g., rise in fascism and White supremacy, cataclysmic environmental events, poisoning of an entire community's water, increased militarism of police and mass incarcerations, especially of People of Color) (https://www.ted.com/talks/naomi_klein_how_shocking_events_can_spark_positive_change). She explores examples of coordinated and sustained responses to these events and identifies two significant ingredients for what she called "deep transformation"—imagination and organization. Imagination refers to our ability to visualize what a more positive future might look like. Klein notes that when we have a vision of what we expect or what could be, large-scale change is more likely than when we act only in opposition, saying no to offenses without clarity about how things could be better. She suggests, "When large scale crises hit us and we are confronted with the need to leap to somewhere safer, there isn't any agreement of what that place is. And leaping without a destination looks a lot like jumping up and down." Often we think of jumping into action, similar to Klein's ingredient of organization. The strategies section of this workbook will present tools to do that. But first, we want to focus on the first ingredient, imagination. In this section, we have several activities to help you tap into your sources of passion as well as to help you focus that passion for positive change and action.

The first four activities are designed to help clarify the motivations and energy that are part of your driving force to engage in social action. In Activity 2.1, you will create a visual image representing what is important to you. In Activity 2.2, you will reflect on who has influenced you and who has shaped your passion for justice. Activity 2.3 taps into the life lessons you have learned, rules you live by, and values and beliefs that guide you. These three activities have been chosen to tap into different aspects or ways of being: your unspoken sense, your emotional connection to learning from others, and an understanding of what shapes your rules for living. Activity 2.4 distills your values into words that capture what you hold dear because understanding the "why" can guide "how" we engage more effectively in social action.

### ACTIVITY 2.1

## Finding What's Most Important

**You will need:** A sheet of paper at least 8.5" × 11" (used paper is fine); scissors, glue stick or tape, magazines, photos, newspapers, and anything with images. You can also do this activity electronically (e.g., digital images), if that is a more comfortable medium.

**Part 1:** Think about what is most important to you in your life and what you value, believe in, and engage in. Bring it to life by creating a collage.

In the center of the paper, place words, pictures, and photographs that represent what is most important to you in your life, and what you value, believe in, and engage in. Surround that word with photos, pictures, and words that describe or illustrate what that word means to you and what helps support it.

For example, let's consider what it might look like if you chose to include the word *Love* at the center. Love of family, community, a partner, and humanity. You might choose words to surround the center that you believe support love. For example, you may believe that civil rights, equality, equity, respect, and certain policies or laws promote love. The collage can also include religious symbols and photos of extended family members and community members of different faiths, sexual orientations, immigrants, justice, etc.

Now, it's your turn. Consider what you might choose to be at the center. Write your word in the middle (or use images to represent it) and surround the center with words or images that support and give meaning to that word.

**FIGURE 2.1** "What's important to you" example

**Part 2:** Once you have completed the collage, stand back and look at it.

- What feelings do the images bring up for you?
- With whom would you feel comfortable sharing this collage and your feelings about it?
- What does this tell you about where you would like to direct your energy?
- What social issues or causes are prompted by the images or feelings?
- Can this collage and the images here serve as an anchor and motivation for you if you feel exhausted or discouraged through your process of creating social change? If not, what images might serve that purpose?

We are one of the most important tools we use in social action. What is most important to us, what stokes our fire, and what lights our passion often has roots in those who have inspired us. Taking a moment to reflect on those people who have influenced, inspired, and guided us can help us to ground our work and purpose. It can also be helpful to revisit this later as we discuss how to sustain our efforts and energy. In the activity below, take a few moments to reflect on the people who have inspired you and how that has shaped your action and potential.

## ACTIVITY 2.2

## Heroes and Inspirations

Identify two role models, idols, or heroes. They could be family, ancestors, people in your community, world leaders, or even fictional characters.

- What kind of social action did they engage in, and how did they inspire you?
- What did you learn from them?

## MUNINDER'S HEROES

I come from a Sikh family, and social justice is a large part of my religious upbringing and beliefs. I grew up reading stories about the Sikh Gurus and Sikh history that emphasized faith, family, community strength, taking care of those with fewer resources than ourselves, and a responsibility to fight against oppression. I wanted to emulate the Gurus and their actions as they fought for gender equality, religious freedom, and the elimination of the caste system. I was raised to engage in *seva*, or community service, and help cook or serve food for *langar* (community kitchen) at the *gurdwara* (Sikh place of worship).

As immigrants, my parents engaged in social action in particular ways: my father as a professor who worked to provide academic opportunities for those for whom few opportunities existed and my mother as an artist who painted murals on hospital walls. They instilled in me concepts of respect, honesty, fairness, justice, advocating for others, and fighting for what's right. I remember two of my ma's paintings hung in my room as a child: Dr. Martin Luther King Jr. and President John F. Kennedy. I remember wanting to be like these men because they fought for ideals a young me (and my parents) believed in. I read about them, I read their words, and reflected on their accomplishments. I wanted to be like them but didn't consider anything beyond the idea that they stood for people's rights at an oppressive time. These idols were larger than life. I wanted to be like them, but I didn't know how.

## REBECCA'S ROLE MODELS: VALUES LEARNED

When I think back to the early lessons I received, I think about the values my parents emphasized: fairness, inclusion, sharing, nonviolence, and the importance of questioning authority. My parents emphasized fairness in our daily lives by serving exactly equal portions of dinner regardless of status and ensuring that none of my siblings received more than another. If there were events or celebrations, my mother insisted that everyone should be invited into our home and didn't want anyone to be left out (e.g., everyone in the class, neighbors passing by, international students who could not return home, etc.). During holidays, it felt like anyone who wasn't able to be with their own family was invited to our house. In elementary school, when I was distressed because the girls I normally played with started a game called "war" where everyone was divided up and were plotting against each other, my parents suggested that I say I was a neutral country (of course that didn't go over well with the girls at my school).

My family attended a Catholic church, and my parents emphasized aspects of Catholic social teachings that applied to serving those who had less than we did, including addressing poverty, discrimination, human dignity, pacifism, and critique of capitalism. We went to peace marches at the local university, and Pete Seeger, Bob Dylan, and Joan Baez were the musicians my mother loved. We were involved in an artist community that emphasized imagination, creativity, community building, and expression for good. Cesar Chavez is one of the heroes I remember from my youth as we participated in the lettuce and grape boycotts even though we were far removed from it living in Iowa. The values that were emphasized in my home are firmly rooted in the way I try to live my life.

For a variety of reasons, Rebecca's family functioned relatively independently of other families. For her, social justice was something her parents taught and demonstrated through various actions. The sense of belonging from the artist and church community in which her family engaged was based on shared values. Because they reflected relatively privileged (racially and religiously) communities, this sense of belonging was related to shared interests and beliefs and not visibly shaped by survival in oppressive circumstances. For Muninder, on the other hand, there is a sense of connection and commitment to a shared survival and spiritual community bond. As you reflect on the next few activities, honor and illuminate those positive forces on your life, whether they be lessons, values, spiritual beliefs, or involvement in a community.

Sometimes the most powerful influences on our values and beliefs are those lessons we have been taught throughout our life, sometimes through stories, sayings, parables, *dichos* (sayings), metaphors, and other ways that wisdom was passed on to us by parents, elders, community members, religious leaders, educators, and others. For example, "do unto others as you would have them do unto you," "*dime con quien andas y te diré quien eres*" (tell me who your friends are and I will tell you who you are); and "walk your talk." In Sikhism, we aspire to "live in *Chardi Kala,*" or live in a state of eternal optimism and positivity, even in the face of hardship or oppression. For me (Muninder), it is a central message that my family has passed down to younger generations and it is the primary principle for how I approach life.

In the next activity, recall stories or lessons you were told as a child. These stories guide how we live our lives, including what social justice issues are important to us and how we engage with them, even if it is not clear to you right now how those may have shaped you. Write down what you remember and what these stories mean to you now. Often these stories or lessons are best remembered in the original language through which they were shared, the language of our family in childhood.

## ACTIVITY 2.3

### Stories or Lessons Handed Down

1.   In the left column in the table below, write down at least three stories or lessons you remember.
2.   In the right column, describe how this lesson may have shaped how you aspire to live your life, how you engage with others, and the kind of person you hope to be.

| Story | What Does This Mean to You Now? |
|---|---|
| 1. | |
| 2. | |
| 3. | |
| Other? | |

So far, in this chapter, you have tapped into different aspects that contribute to the person you are now and the energy you bring to justice work. In the next activity, you will summarize values and beliefs that you hold dear; in other words, the spark, kindling, and fuel that guide you to engage in social action.

## ACTIVITY 2.4

### Your Spark, Kindling, and Fuel

1.   Circle all the words below that represent the values and beliefs that guide you or that you hold dear. Remember that this list can be as private as you want, so be honest with yourself.
2.   If you think of any values and beliefs that are not listed that are important for you be sure to add them in the blank boxes.

3. Place an asterisk (*) by the top 8.

| Harmony with people | Communities | Peace * | Passion | Fame |
|---|---|---|---|---|
| Justice | Relationships with animals | Happiness | Romance | Human rights |
| Education * | Relationships with people * | Freedom * | Integrity | Participation in decision making |
| Aesthetics | Wisdom | Religion/God * | Humility | Patriotism |
| Economic success | Safety | Spirituality | Achievement | Physical health |
| Fairness | Health | Kindness * | Recognition | Pleasure |
| Balance with nature | Family | Creativity | Solitude | Independence |
| Honesty * | Security | Loyalty * | Power | Interdependence |
| Other? | | | | |

The activities you completed in this chapter are intended to encourage you to connect with important aspects of yourself that can help you shape how you engage in social action and how you sustain that action during difficult times. There are so many different issues, events, and problems daily that need to be addressed in our world. Yet, there is only so much time and energy. Whereas Activity 2.4 identifies broad values, Activities 2.5, 2.6, and 2.7 move to the next step by focusing on the issues you care about, identifying what keeps you from acting on them, and helping you begin to create your message.

Now that you have identified some of the core values and beliefs that may spark your passion and commitment, the next activity aims to summarize how you use that passion. Activity 2.5 asks you to consider social justice issues that arise in your community, nation, or world, and to identify what you care about and want to focus on.

## ACTIVITY 2.5

### Where Do You Focus Your Fire? Issues You Care About

1. Circle all the words that represent issues that your care about.
2. If there are issues you care about that are missing, be sure to add them in the blank boxes.
3. Place an asterisk (*) by the 3 issues that are most important to you.

| | | | | |
|---|---|---|---|---|
| Protecting the environment | Economic justice | Immigration rights | Refugee rights | Religious rights (and freedom from discrimination) |
| Animal rights | Ending poverty | Education access | Global peace | Access to job training |
| Civil rights | Employment rights | Health care access | Rights of currently and formerly incarcerated | Social justice |
| Antiracism | Digital divide and access to technology | Housing access | LGBTQ rights | Disability rights |
| Anti-sexism | Rights of older adults | Victims' rights (sexual assault, etc.) | Trans and other gender rights | Rights of undocumented persons |
| Indigenous people's rights | Reproductive rights | Prison industrial complex | Children's rights | |

# Getting Over Barriers That May Keep You From Action

Barriers—real and perceived—are important to consider because they often prevent us from engaging, or even trying to engage, in the work. However, barriers can be unpacked to understand what lies underneath them and help you decide which barriers are worth tackling.

Depending on who we are and what our social location is (i.e., our identities and how those identities are positioned in society related to access to resources), barriers may be larger or smaller. Some barriers can be more easily overcome with privilege (i.e., access to money, power, or freedom from harassment, etc.) and privilege can act as a buffer against negative repercussions that might arise. For example, if you are interested in engaging in advocacy that requires money, it is easier to engage if you have financial flexibility. If your income is essential to your family's well-being, and speaking out might threaten your job, you have a very real barrier to engaging in certain kinds of social justice work. Other barriers may be more psychological (for example, fear) or interpersonal (objections from family, for instance). These can often keep us from taking action. For example, a lack of confidence in developing relationships with people in a community different from your own may stop you from getting involved.

It can be helpful to consider ways around barriers and recognize when a barrier is unlikely to be overcome, at least for now. Most barriers can be transformed to become "stepping stones" or sub-goals rather than a force that prevents us from moving. To use a metaphor of a wall as a barrier, we could come to a wall blocking the path and sit down to say we are done. Or we can sit down and think about whether it is important to get to the other side of the wall, and if so, how might we find ways to go around or over the wall or even take it down entirely.

There are numerous barriers we encounter in our efforts to work toward social justice. It is important to acknowledge them and then take a look at what we can do about the barriers. This next activity is designed to get you started by taking a look at what gets in your way when you move toward action for issues you care about. Thinking about what you can do instead of what you can't do is essential.

## ACTIVITY 2.6

### Barriers—What Makes It Hard to Act?

Take a minute and close your eyes. Reflect on the issues that you identified in Activity 2.5. Think about the times you want to take action but don't. What keeps you from doing it? In the three sections below, consider these barriers. Some may be logistical or circumstantial barriers (for example, you are unable to take time off work), some may be internal (ways of thinking, for instance), and some may be interpersonal (for example, conflicts with people we are close to).

**Part 1: What Makes It Difficult to Act?**

| External, logistical, or circumstances |
| --- |
| —time or money |
| Psychological or internal barriers |
| "One person won't fix the problem |
| Relational or interpersonal barriers |
| - fear of what others will think <br> -shy |

Many of these barriers and challenges may actually be choices. Acknowledging this helps us to begin to be more conscious about the choices we make, and we may decide to act anyway. Or it may help us to think about ways to address the issue using an alternative approach. For example, if we are making choices about whether to spend time with family rather than going to a social action event and that feels very important for the sustainability of our family, then we might consider alternatives to contributing to that social action issue instead of attending this event. Or, we may consider inviting our family to participate in the event. The point is that there is value in acknowledging our circumstances and choices before considering alternatives. For the second part of this activity, choose one of the barriers above and answer the following questions.

**Part 2: Getting Past the Barrier**

| |
|---|
| Barrier: Fear |
| If you ignored this barrier and acted anyway, what would happen? <br> —either rejection or praise, or nothing |
| Are there actions you could take to make this less of a barrier? <br> Yes, practice |
| Is there an alternative way you could address the injustice or issue you care about? <br> anonamously |

Now, reflect on how this barrier shapes whether and how you take action.

- What is real about the barrier?
- What can be changed?
- Is there another road you can take?

Throughout the rest of this workbook, you may notice that barriers come up in your mind. We encourage you to acknowledge them, even write them down, and then consider the choices you can make about whether those barriers will keep you from acting or may simply shape the way you choose to act. When we do choose to act, having support from others can help minimize barriers as well as strengthen the actions we take. When we have difficulty communicating what is important to us and why we are making the choices that we do, it is harder for us to get support. In the next section, you will begin creating your messaging about a social justice issue. This can help make your action stronger as well as help others understand your issue, support you, and potentially join you in action.

## Clarity and Creating Your Message

By this point, you have identified and reflected on what you value, what you believe in, and what you care about. You can prepare yourself for many of the activities that follow by beginning to develop a succinct description about what you are committed to and what you'd like to see happen. You should be able to communicate this in an "elevator speech," a short (one minute or less) script that answers, "What do you do and why should I care?" inviting the listener to ask for more information (Association for Library Service to Children; http://www.ala.org/everyday-advocacy/speak-out/write-elevator-speech).

There are a number of models for this type of speech, yet common threads include: introducing yourself and where you are coming from; the issue, and why it is important; what you are doing about the issue; and what you want from the listener. We will guide you in developing an elevator speech, step by step, building throughout the workbook. In the following activity, you will develop the first parts of an elevator speech: creating an engaging introduction to one of the issues you care about. As you progress through the workbook, you will add to this speech, and by the end you will have a succinct, clear, and actionable message. This message can help you stay focused on your intent, communicate the importance of your issue and engage others, and even help you to overcome barriers you might encounter.

---

### ACTIVITY 2.7

#### Beginning Your "Elevator Speech"

1. Introduce yourself by name, position, and place (one sentence). For example, "I am Maria Davis, a student at Acme University (or a community member in Everytown)."
2. What is the issue, and why is it important to you personally? Why do you care about it? (This should be no more than one or two sentences.)

Once you have crafted this, try it out on family and friends. What do they think? Do they understand what you are trying to convey about your issue and why you believe it is important?

---

Now you have the beginning of your elevator speech, your concise message about what you care about. You will continue to develop it throughout the workbook, integrating your compelling message to engage others and keep yourself engaged. For the next step, we introduce a comprehensive model (the S-quad model) created to help you reflect on four areas that can help you engage in, and sustain, social action. As we work through the model in the next several chapters, you will continue to add to your elevator speech as well as to the knowledge, skills, and strategies that will help you to take action and invite others to join you.

# section 2

Taking Action

section **2**

# chapter three

# Introduction to the S⁴ (S-Quad)

## Strength, Solidarity, Strategy, and Sustainability

Strength      Solidarity

Sustainability      Strategy

As mentioned earlier, in the face of increasingly challenging political and social times, many of us struggle to stay positive in living out our values and acting on what we believe is right. Although we (Muninder and Rebecca) have been writing and teaching about advocacy and social justice for almost two decades, we have still found it difficult to feel anchored, effective, and consistent in our actions.

A couple of years ago, I (Rebecca) was asked to give a talk in Greece about social justice in counseling psychology. I felt nervous that the work I had done in the United States might not be relevant or culturally sensitive to the complexities that professionals in Greece were facing. I reflected on the lessons I had learned throughout my professional life as well as the challenges. There were four major themes that seemed to guide successful action: Strength, Solidarity, Strategy, and Sustainability (four Ss or S-quad). Muninder and I are using these four areas of reflection and action to help lead us back to our paths and remind us how to continue to work toward social justice more effectively. They also remind us to try to be realistic about our lives and be better contributors to the social action efforts already going on in our communities. Although we are still challenged to stay positive and effective given the enormity of issues and injustice, they have served as helpful reminders and anchor us. We humbly share this with you and hope that you find the process helpful as well.

In the S-quad approach to social action, the first theme, Strength, emphasizes that despite our frequent lack of confidence to change the world, we do have strengths and skills that are valuable for addressing social justice issues. This also includes resources, knowledge, and experience that we bring to the table. The second area, Solidarity, reflects the power of our relationships with others. This is important for camaraderie and, more importantly, solidarity points to the essential place of allyship (or "accomplicity") and humility in acknowledging and learning from other folks who are directly affected by the issues that we are concerned about. The third area for reflection and action, Strategy, embodies the importance of being informed and strategic in confronting injustice. We have sometimes been reminded of this lesson the hard way, after acting quickly without a clear plan or without understanding possible consequences. The emphasis on strategy comes from the wisdom of our many mentors who teach that large-scale change requires a multifaceted approach, often over a long span of time. The fourth area for reflection and action, Sustainability, focuses on sustaining ourselves in the process, and the importance of balancing our roles in our families, our health, and our jobs with the time and effort needed for action to address injustice. For example, after decades of struggling with chronic health issues, I (Rebecca) have come to realize that if my health is compromised, I am not able to help or contribute to social action in meaningful ways. I have priorities in my everyday life beyond social action that cannot be sacrificed, for my own well-being, for the sake of my family, and ultimately for survival. Thus, I have to be conscious of how to balance attention to those important areas with attention and action for the social justice issues I am committed to.

These four areas of reflection and action, S-quad, all work together to help provide focus and strengthen action toward social justice in the face of challenging times. In this workbook, we offer a process for exploring and developing a social action plan as well as suggest knowledge and skill development that may be helpful. The S-quad model provides food for thought and avenues that may help you to activate in meaningful and sustainable ways. It is our hope that these activities will help you in your efforts, whether you are just starting or have been an activist and advocate for a long time.

# chapter four

# Strengths, Assets, and Resources

## What You Have Right Now in Your Toolbox

Strength

Several years ago, Alicia Garza, one of the founders of the Black Lives Matter (BLM) movement in Oakland, California, responded to a caller during a radio interview who described feeling overwhelmed by all the injustice they saw. The caller asked for advice about what to do. Garza shared wisdom that had been shared with her: "Figure out what you do well, then do it ferociously" (paraphrased). With this approach, the task of social action becomes more manageable and immediate. This also fits with what we know about job success and finding a work path that builds on what one has to offer. The statement reminds us that we already know much that can be put into action right now. This idea inspires the power of finding and using our strengths to spark and drive the social justice work we can do.

You can think about the S-quad model as a toolbox and your Strengths as the tools you already have that can be used to take action. Strengths are a combination of your skills, knowledge, and expertise. We also encourage you to think about the resources you have access to in terms of actual material things as well as relationships with other people who can bring skills, knowledge, and resources to the project. You bring strengths and resources to your social justice efforts whether in your personal life or in the way you do your job.

The following activities are designed to help you create an inventory of tools you have access to when taking action. They are also intended to help you think about using some of these strengths to nurture relationships for Solidarity, developing Strategies, and ensuring your personal Sustainability and wellness in the process. We will start by focusing on the skills you have now, perhaps used in one area, that may be applied in a variety of areas.

# Skills

When we think of skills that are helpful in pursuing social change, it is important to consider all types, including functional skills (i.e., transferable skills like people skills or being bilingual) and technical skills (e.g., building websites, car repair, developing curriculum). To really tap into all that you have to offer, it is important for you to consider even the skills that seemingly have nothing to do with the cause that you are working on. Transferable or functional skills are things you do in one setting that could be used in a different setting or a different way. For example, if you like making schedules for you or your family, you may be good at creating timelines and schedules for getting a social action project done. The following activities ask you to think about the strengths and skills you use currently or have used in the past, regardless of the setting or purpose.

## ACTIVITY 4.1

### Strengths—What Do Others See in You?

Sometimes others (individuals close to us and strangers) see our strengths better than we can. These strengths may be values and beliefs that guide our actions and behaviors or they could be skills and knowledge. Strengths can also shine through as personality traits and ways of interacting with others. In this activity, you will reach out to others who know you to develop a picture of your strengths.

1. Ask two or three people you know and trust to help identify your strengths and list these out. For some of us, it may be awkward to ask others about our positive qualities. If that is true for you, there are a few ways you can do this; for example:
    a. What do you think I'm good at?
    b. If I asked you to write a letter of recommendation for me, what would you say?
2. Once you have created this list, based on what others have shared about you, reflect on whether you have seen these strengths in yourself?
3. How can you build on these strengths?

Strengths provide a foundation for how we operate naturally or more easily. Identifying these can help reveal various ways that you may be able to support a cause. This second activity asks you to rate how comfortable you feel using a range of different skills regardless of the type of setting or goal.

## ACTIVITY 4.2

### What Do I Do Well?

Below are examples of different types of skills to get you started. Consider each of the following skills and mark an **x** in the boxes indicating how comfortable you feel with each skill. This is not an exhaustive list (there are many, many others), so feel free to add your other skills if you think they are missing. It may help you to think about previous jobs, hobbies, training, or anything where you have applied skills. For example, if you feel like speaking in person to strangers is an area of strength for you, you would put an **x** in the box under A. If there is a skill area that is not mentioned within a skill set, write it in the "other skill" box.

A- area of strength
B- feel comfortable using; could improve
C- don't feel comfortable but would like to develop
D- don't feel comfortable and don't want to develop

| Skill Set | Skill | A | B | C | D |
|---|---|---|---|---|---|
| *Speaking* | in person to strangers | | X | | |
| | in person to people I know | X | | | |
| | to legislators or businesses | | | X | |
| | to media (e.g., reporters, etc.) | | | | X |
| | by phone to strangers | | | X | |
| | by phone to people I know | X | | | |
| | one-on-one | X | | | |
| | in groups | | X | | |
| | when teaching | | X | | |
| | in conversation | | X | | |
| | to children | X | | | |
| | to adults | | X | | |
| | to community members | | | X | |
| | to professionals | | | X | |
| | Other speaking skill? | | | | |

| Working With Groups | Skill | A | B | C | D |
|---|---|---|---|---|---|
| | Resolving conflicts | | | X | |
| | Working on a team | X | | | |
| | Facilitating groups | | X | | |
| | Motivating others | X | | | |
| | Leading | X | | | |
| | Following | X | | | |
| | Listening respectfully | X | | | |
| | Negotiating | | X | | |
| | Organizing groups of people | | X | | |
| | Supervising | X | | | |
| | Training or educating | X | | | |
| | Other skill working with groups? | | | | |
| **Technical Skills** | **Skill** | **A** | **B** | **C** | **D** |
| | Using social media | X | | | |
| | Creating and maintaining websites, blogs | | | X | |
| | Creating podcasts | | | X | |
| | Setting up and managing sound equipment | | | X | |
| | Using video recording equipment | | X | | |
| | Other technical skill? | | | | |
| **Organizational Skills** | **Skill** | **A** | **B** | **C** | **D** |
| | Event planning | X | | | |
| | Fundraising | X | | | |
| | Planning (e.g., timelines, project plans, etc.) | X | | | |
| | Other organizational skill? | | | | |
| **Working with Information** | **Skill** | **A** | **B** | **C** | **D** |
| | Researching information | | | X | |
| | Budgeting | | X | | |
| | Tracking information in a spreadsheet | | | X | |
| | Other skill working with information? | | | | |

| Artistic Skills | Skill | A | B | C | D |
|---|---|---|---|---|---|
| | Creating posters and banners | X | | | |
| | Painting murals | X | | | |
| | Musical abilities | | | X | |
| | Poetry or spoken word | | | X | |
| | Performance art | | X | | |
| | Other artistic skill? | | | | |
| Writing Skills | Skill | A | B | C | D |
| | Writing persuasively | X | | | |
| | Writing letters | | X | | |
| | Writing legal documents | | | X | |
| | Writing technical or academic reports | | | X | |
| | Editing | | | X | |
| | Other writing skill? | | | | |
| Mechanical or Construction Skills | Skill | A | B | C | D |
| | Mechanical skills (e.g., fixing things) | | X | | |
| | Construction (e.g., building things) | | | X | |
| | Other mechanical or construction skill? | | | | |
| Language Skills | Skill | A | B | C | D |
| | Bilingual or multilingual | | | X | |
| | Other language skill? | | | | |
| Other Skills | Skill | A | B | C | D |
| | | | | | |
| | | | | | |
| | | | | | |

Circle rows A, B, and C together. These are skills that you have or want to use. Add the number of As, Bs, and Cs, and note the sheer number of skills that exist or are a possibility. Add a star next to any skill that you feel comfortable using for a social justice issue that you are committed to. In the spaces below, make some notes about patterns you notice or specifics about the skills (e.g., in person, by phone, with strangers, with people you

know, with adults, with children, etc.) as well as skills you would like to strengthen.

_____

_____

_____

Later, we will discuss D and how you might develop these skills or seek out others who may be important to work with as they have the skills you don't have.

The skills you have identified above reflect one aspect of the strengths you can use for social action and may also help you later as you consider how to connect with communities, as well as the social action strategies that might work well for you. There are other areas of strengths that are important to consider as well.

## Personal Qualities

In addition to transferable or functional skills, personal qualities reflect a different type of strength we can bring to social action. Personal qualities reflect who we are, our preferences in how we interact with others, as well as how we approach the world and our way through it. When we are in situations that require personal qualities that we have not developed well, we often struggle, feel out of place, or feel frustrated. Some examples of personal qualities include conveying compassion for others, preferring to work alone, feeling energized working with others, being reflective and observant, and being engaged or enthusiastic. We mention personal qualities because they are often about HOW we approach connecting with others in solidarity or playing our part in social action. It is important to know these things about ourselves. In her TED Talk about how introverts make good activists, Sarah Corbett points out that often we think of activism as requiring intensive interaction with people, yet there are important and creative strategies that take a different approach (https://www.ted.com/talks/sarah_corbett_activism_needs_introverts). She also notes that although it can be good to stretch beyond your comfort zone, too much of that too quickly can result in burnout. Yes, we can grow and stretch into qualities that may be less developed, still, social change needs all kinds of people and all kinds of personal qualities. It will be easier if you are able to utilize those that come naturally to you. Before moving on, think about the personal qualities you have (sometimes it is easier to think about how people describe you). As you continue in the workbook, keep these qualities in mind as strengths you bring to your work.

# Knowledge

Knowledge that we have developed over time and experience may be helpful, sometimes in unexpected ways. Whereas "skills" are about knowing "how" to do something, knowledge is knowing "about" something and holding some type of information. For example, "knowledge" might be understanding how local elections work, how bail bonds work, customs in various cultural and religious communities, where to find inexpensive art supplies, how to navigate public transportation, etc. Other examples might include understanding human behavior, marketing, how to access public assistance, legal processes, local history, zoning processes, economics, or financial matters. Some of this knowledge may come from your professional training, occupation, what you do in your free time, or simply personal experience.

Before beginning the next exercise, it may be helpful to consider the example below.

## EXAMPLE

### Reflections of Muninder and Rebecca

In our professional roles as psychologists and professors who educate counselors in training, we both bring knowledge about the field of counseling and psychology, including mental health issues in schools, communities, and higher education. We know how universities operate and what criteria individuals may need to get into their respective programs. Knowledge outside of professional realms is just as important as knowledge within. For example, as a Sikh woman of Indian descent, Muninder knows about the customs of her religion and culture and what values underpin them. She knows good Indian restaurants in New York and gurdwaras as well as the "vibe" of each. She knows how to play the harmonium (an Indian instrument) and speaks Punjabi. As a salsa dancer, Muninder knows the steps to salsa, knows the good salsa socials in New York, speaks some Spanish, and knows some of the musicians. Muninder brings particular sources of knowledge with her. Rebecca was raised Catholic and so has some knowledge of how that organization works and the rituals associated with it. She was also raised by artistic parents and had many opportunities to express herself and use tools and materials such as clay, paint, wood, and other media. She has developed basic Spanish-speaking skills and engaged with numerous different cultural communities in the San Francisco Bay Area. She has been committed to working with homeless individuals and understands the wide range of reasons and stories of people who find themselves in that situation. She commutes by train and bus daily and so understands how to get around using public transportation as well as interact with a wide range of people on a daily basis who also use public transportation.

It is likely this next exercise will not uncover all the areas of knowledge you hold, but we hope that it will help you start thinking about the wealth of knowledge you have acquired that may be useful in advocacy endeavors.

---

### ACTIVITY 4.3

### You Are Becoming an Expert

Think about the things you are knowledgeable about in each type of experience. Note various sources of knowledge from your jobs (paid and unpaid), formal and informal education, volunteerism, and even leisure activities. This knowledge and expertise can be useful to engage in social action.

**Part 1:** What professional knowledge did you use or gain in the various jobs or volunteer positions you have held? (For example, as a mechanic you may know about various engines; as a tax return preparer you may know different forms needed, depending on a person's financial circumstance.) **Think about your most recent jobs, and list all of the knowledge areas that come to mind:**

Job 1

_____

_____

_____

Job 2

_____

_____

_____

Job 3

_____

_____

_____

**Part 2:** What personal knowledge do you have based on community activities? This can include leisure activities (for example, if you enjoy attending live music concerts, you may know the best places in your community to enjoy live music inexpensively, perhaps even places that would allow for a benefit concert for a cause. Another example might be participating with your religious community). **Think about things you enjoy doing and the knowledge you gain from those activities or the knowledge you need in order to engage in those activities. List at least three interests below and the knowledge areas related to them:**

Interest 1:

Interest 2:

Interest 3:

# Resources

Other important parts of your toolbox include resources such as actual material and nonmaterial things, as well as relationships with others who might have resources, skills, or knowledge. Doing an inventory of what we have and what we need is a good way to begin to look at what could be available even if we don't know yet whether it might be useful or how we would use it. Applying this to the idea of a toolbox for social action, if each of us considers the resources we have, then when we come together as a team, these can become shared resources for a collective cause.

There are several types of resources that are needed to engage in social action, including those that are tangible (e.g., financial, real estate, craft supplies, food, meeting space, or access to any of these) and those that are intangible (e.g., time, flexibility, social capital, relationships with people).

**EXAMPLE**

## Rebecca's Use of Resources to Contribute

The Sogorea Te Land Trust is an urban, Indigenous women–led community organization that facilitates the return of Chochenyo and Karkin Ohlone lands in the San Francisco Bay Area to Indigenous stewardship. In collaboration with Indian People Organizing for Change, the organization was holding a rally to draw attention to efforts to save sacred land and shellmounds from being developed into a shopping mall. The rally was scheduled for a Friday, and I knew I would not be able to attend due to a previous commitment. However, I learned through the organization's social media page that a member of another organization (Showing Up for Racial Justice [SURJ], a local chapter of a national organization created by White people to facilitate action and challenge institutional and systemic racism) was holding a sign-making event in her home to prepare signs for the rally. The organizer provided art supplies along with some sample signs for inspiration. I brought a bag of apples to share and we made about 50 signs and used up almost all the supplies. At some point, it occurred to me that the art supplies had not magically appeared, and I'm sure they were not cheap. I had craft paint and many markers at home left over from the years of art projects with my kids, but it hadn't occurred to me to bring them. I decided the least I could do was contribute some cash and asked the host if that would be okay. She responded with an emphatic "Oh yes! That would be great!" A couple of other volunteers then also offered to contribute.

This story illustrates resources that were both tangible and intangible (resources are underlined below). The sign-making event was made possible because the organizer took the time to create it to support the Sogorea Te Land Trust using social media and her connections with SURJ and the Sogorea Te Land Trust. She consulted with Sogorea Te leaders to ensure that the signs and the event would be helpful and appropriate for them. The event was held in the backyard of her landlord's house (she rented a small cottage behind the house); the landlord gave her permission to do so. She purchased art supplies and snacks using her own money. As a sign maker, the resources I had were the time and flexibility to participate, transportation to get to the house (it was about a 30-minute drive), apples, and cash. I also have access to the Internet and a social media account. Bringing food and snacks to share is usually a good idea as it is often a culturally appropriate gesture as well as practical contribution. The next time, I can also contribute unused art supplies that I have sitting in my garage.

In this next activity, you will identify the tangible and intangible resources that you have which can be useful tools in social action either now, or at some point in the future.

ACTIVITY 4.4

### Resources: "I Have It! Or I Know Where I Can Find It"

In the following prompts, brainstorm some ideas about resources you have or have access to. You may be able to create a nice general list now, and then later in the workbook, or when you are faced with an event or potential action, you may realize you have even more resources specific to that situation.

**Tangible resources** (e.g., computer, printer, furniture, space, information, financial resources)

_____

_____

_____

**Intangible resources** (e.g., time, flexibility, connections, speaking multiple languages, physical or emotional strength)

_____

_____

_____

Describe a couple of examples of how you have used these resources in the past to address issues you care about:

_____

_____

_____

You may be able to think of a number of examples of people who have approached their social action using a combination of their skills, knowledge, and resources. One example is Jennifer Mendelsohn, a genealogist who responded to increasingly hostile rhetoric about immigrants by publicizing the immigration histories of outspoken anti-immigration politicians and public figures. She created their family trees, including the immigration stories of their family, demonstrating that the very immigration policy objected to by the public figure is the reason they were originally able to enter and stay in the United States (https://www.cnn.com/2018/01/24/us/immigration-resistance-genealogy-jennifer-mendelsohn-trnd/index.html). Another example is one I (Rebecca) encountered on a flight about a year ago. A woman sitting next to me on a plane noticed a book I was reading about social action, and our conversation turned to her story. She and her partner had worked for decades creating documentaries to educate the public about environmental issues, yet they had begun to feel like the message wasn't as far reaching as it needed to be. They decided to begin work on a book that would address environmental issues but through the context of mixology and cocktails. They contacted well-known mixologists and asked them to create signature cocktails related to an environmental issue related to the drink (e.g., a

Sinking Manhattan to expose the dangers of melting polar ice caps). Each chapter would contain the cocktail recipe as well as information about the environmental issue related to that cocktail. As we talked further, she also described another project they were working on—a musical—that grew out of their continued commitment to civil rights and freedom for the Tibetan people. The musical was about two women, one Tibetan and one Chinese, who are stuck on a rooftop in Los Angeles and find a way to communicate with each other, gaining compassion and understanding and breaking down barriers. The woman sitting next to me on the plane explained that she had never written a musical (or a book), but with the connections and the passion they had, they were branching out, using their skills in a different way.

At this point, it will be helpful to summarize the work you have done to identify some of your strengths. In the activity below, briefly list the top skills, knowledge, and resources you can use to engage in social action.

## ACTIVITY 4.5

### Summary of Your Skills, Knowledge, and Resources

| Skills | Knowledge | Resources |
|--------|-----------|-----------|
|        |           |           |
|        |           |           |
|        |           |           |
|        |           |           |
|        |           |           |
|        |           |           |

You will revisit this summary multiple times throughout the workbook. For example, when we get to the Strategies section, knowing your skills, knowledge, and resources can help you to know how to contribute to specific approaches. Further, if an issue calls for a strategy that feels outside your comfort zone, you may recognize that it could be an area to further develop additional skills and knowledge. This is an important start, yet there are several other additional areas of strength to consider first.

## Strength and Positionality: Who I Am, Where I Am in Relation to Others, and What I Look Like Makes a Difference

Strengths we have not yet fully explored are those you have gained through your experiences in the world given who you are and who the world perceives you to be. *Positionality* refers to where you are in relation to others given your cultural background, experiences, and identities within the society in which you live and interact. Because our society is shaped by social, historical, and political forces, who we are is influenced by the identities we hold and what they mean to us as well as what they mean to others. For example, positionality in relation to race in the United States is shaped by the country's social, political, and economic history. Since the invasion of the American continents by White Europeans, individuals with White European heritage have held political, economic, and social power (for complexities regarding the history of "Whiteness" in the United States, read David R. Roediger's 2018 book *Working Toward Whiteness*). People of other ethnic and national descent also have positionality that is influenced and shaped by historical and political forces as well as existing privilege and power structures within the United States. Immigration status, skin color, economic and educational resources, and many other factors reflect our relationship to others and the power and access we have. The United States is used here as an example, but every country has a history of inclusion, exclusion, power, privilege, and oppression. Our comment in the beginning of the workbook, that some of the workbook is focused on U.S. structures, is an example of our positionality. This positionality shapes our experiences and the systems that impact us. Some of what we know and write about is applicable outside the United States, yet our frame from within the United States must be acknowledged.

Pamela Hays (1996) used the acronym ADRESSING (later referred to as ADDRESSING) (Hays, 2008) to outline the various identities that make up our positionality and reflect the extent to which those identities: 1) benefit from societal privilege (receive unearned advantages based on our membership in an identity group); or 2) face systemic and individual oppression (receive unjust treatment or be blocked from resources due to membership in an identity group). The identities that Hays lists include our age, disability (developmental and acquired) status, religion, ethnicity and race, socioeconomic status, sexual orientation, indigenous heritage, national origin, and gender. Even if you may think these identities don't mean much to you, it is certain that your experience is influenced by the way society (e.g., economic, social, and political systems) and people perceive those aspects of your identity and thus affect the treatment and opportunities you receive. Most of us who hold privileges are not even aware that on a daily basis, we benefit from that privilege. In fact, because privilege reflects the dominant group (historically numerical and political majority), if our identity reflects one that holds privilege, it is easy to assume that these are not privileges and that everyone receives the same opportunities. Often when a person is not aware of their privilege (or even when they are aware), they may not notice oppression as often as it occurs because they don't experience it directly.

## EXAMPLE

### Rebecca's Reflection on Identity and Privilege

I am a White cisgender woman (cisgender means that my appearance is basically consistent with what society expects a woman to look like). Thus, I benefit in numerous ways from this White identity because of the history of White people in the U.S. For example, historically, White people had access to education, loans, and housing free from discrimination based on race. The movie *13th* does a good job of identifying the historical roots of current-day racism and its impact on Black and White individuals and communities. In fact, there are ongoing investigations showing that the impact of racism continues today for People of Color in employment, banking, loans, law enforcement, health care, etc.

As a woman, I have often received assistance with physical tasks, been talked to in simplistic terms, and been subjected to sexual harassment and coercion, due to the way society treats women according to traditionally held gender roles. So in that way, I have less gender privilege than men. As a cisgender woman, although I have never identified with many of society's expectations of femininity, I am basically accepted because I look, more or less, the way this society envisions a woman "should" look. In that sense, I receive privileges that people whose gender identity does not match what society expects (for example, trans people, people who identify as neither male or female, or people who identify as both male and female). We are complex people with different influences and aspects of who we are; some aspects are visible, others are not.

In the following activity, think about these different aspects of your identity, how they influence the ways you see yourself as well as the ways others perceive you. This reflection will help you further develop self-awareness and engage in social action in a more authentic way.

## ACTIVITY 4.6

### Identities That Make Us Who We Are

Using Hays's ADDRESSING model, think about each of the identity dimensions: **age, disability** (developmental and acquired), **religion, ethnicity and race, socioeconomic status, sexual orientation, indigenous heritage, national origin, and gender.**

In the chart below, add a brief description of how you relate to each identity dimension and the influences on each of those identities. For example, for age, consider what your actual age means to you and others, how it is related to experiences of oppression or privilege, and how society considers your generation (e.g., stereotypes like "millennials are liberal but lazy"). For example, Rebecca may write this for age: I am 56 years old; I am often recognized as someone who has life experience, yet because of my age, there may be age discrimination when applying for certain jobs and I may be excluded from certain groups or conversations. Because of the years I have lived, I have seen, and hopefully learned from, the civil rights movement, the women's movement, historical involvement of the United States in other countries, changes in political and economic policy, etc.

| Identity Dimension | Description of Your Relationship to That Identity | Privileged Group* |
|---|---|---|
| **A**ge | | 30–60 years old |
| **D**isability (physical, sensory, cognitive, developmental, learning, or psychological) | | No disability |
| **R**eligion | | Christian and secular |
| **E**thnicity and Race | | White (especially of western European descent) |
| **S**ocioeconomic Status | | Upper and middle income/class, including holding college degrees |

| Sexual Orientation | | Heterosexual |
|---|---|---|
| **I**ndigenous Heritage (belonging to original peoples of a land) | | No indigenous heritage (or very little) |
| **N**ational Origin (country where you were born) | | U.S.-born (even more so if your parents are U.S.-born) |
| **G**ender | | Cisgender male |

* Privilege group is shaped by the cultural lens of the society we live in. Here we have used the United States. The privilege markers we have identified in this table reflect those suggested by Hays but are slightly adapted given our contexts and purposes.

Reflecting on various aspects of our identity and what those might mean in terms of our experiences with power, privilege, and oppression allows us to have more complex insights and opportunities to understand the world in particular ways. It is important to consider that, given these identities (especially the visible ones), we represent something to the people we encounter. This is often most obvious to people who experience discrimination because they have to navigate a world run by people who have a lot of societal privilege. Whereas, when we identify, look, or act like others in the mainstream cultures, we don't necessarily notice or reflect on our difference, and this can impact how we engage with others and in social action. In the next exercise, think about the different aspects of your identity and what they may mean when you engage with others. Awareness of how we use our identities and how our identities influence our interactions is important as we work to expand our social mosaic or network of relationships. It will also be useful information for our discussion of Solidarity and Strategies later in the workbook.

We all have both visible and invisible identities that others encounter when they meet or interact with us. How aware are we of these? In the next activity, we use Rebecca's identities as examples throughout so you can see how this activity can unfold.

### ACTIVITY 4.7

## How Others Perceive Us Makes a Difference — Inside/Outside

For each of the identity aspects in the above ADDRESSING activity, imagine meeting a new person for the first time. What aspects of your identity are most recognized?

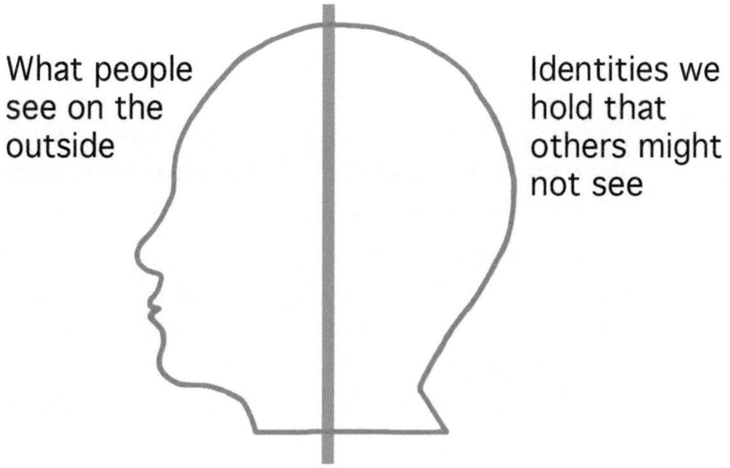

What people see on the outside

Identities we hold that others might not see

**FIGURE 4.1**   Our identities: What is visible to others and what is not

1.   Write your identity dimensions on the left side (the front of the face). Although this may change somewhat depending on whom you are interacting with, for now, think about the aspects of your identity that are most visible.

*Example: My (Rebecca's) skin is White and a bit wrinkly. I dress and wear my hair like many women within the United States. I walk and use my arms, legs, eyes, and mouth much like most people I encounter (I do not have visible physical disabilities). Therefore, I believe the identities that are most visible to people I encounter are as a White, cisgender woman (I look the way U.S. society expects a woman to look), middle-aged, and mostly physically able-bodied. What those identities mean to others depends on the meaning they attach to what they see.*

2.   Now, for those aspects of your identity that are important to you but may not be visible to others, write those on the right side of the head (the back side of the head).

*Example: I (Rebecca) am Canadian but grew up in the United States. I was raised Catholic (but do not identify as Catholic or religious). I am in a long-term, heterosexual relationship. I am not aware of any indigenous heritage in my family. Two aspects of my identity may vary in terms of visibility to others: disability status and socioeconomic status. I have chronic migraines, sometimes daily for weeks at a time. During those times, even when medicated, I may be disoriented, experience sensory overload, have difficulty focusing, memory issues, and other effects. People close to me can often identify when I am having migraines. Although others may not recognize this, it influences the way I interact with them in a relatively significant way. Perception of my socioeconomic status is another dimension that varies, depending on where I am, how I am dressed, and how I interact with others.*

3. Once you have drawn the picture of your visible and invisible identities, think a bout how this might change in terms of whom you interact with and where you interact. Make some notes about your insights.

   *Example: When I (Rebecca), as a White person, interact with other White people in a context where most people are White and the purpose of us coming together is not related to race, then the other White people may not be conscious of seeing me as a White person. White people generally grow up experiencing Whiteness as the norm and thus may only consciously notice race when someone is different from them (sometimes not even then). If I am in a group where there are very few White people, others in the group may be more likely to notice my Whiteness. However, a Person of Color may consciously notice my Whiteness in any context. My Whiteness will mean different things to different people. In other words, the identities and experiences of the person I am talking to will influence the way they interpret my interactions. For some, my Whiteness may feel safe, while others may feel mistrustful because of what other White people have done, or even because of things I might unintentionally do.*

The way we see ourselves and the ways others perceive us shape our interactions, our opportunities, and our relationships. These visible, and invisible, identities can present strengths as well as challenges yet are also somewhat limited in that they don't fully represent who we are. They don't reflect all of the ways that we have learned and engaged in our world or what we bring to what we do.

## What We Have Learned Throughout Our Life

Another area of knowledge is related to our lived experience as a person who has many different roles, holds different identities, or belongs to particular communities (e.g., a person who identifies as Latinx, person with a disability, etc.).

**EXAMPLE**

### Muninder

I am a New Yorker and thus have learned a lot about cities and how to navigate them. I have friends in different boroughs and know how to travel on the subway efficiently and effectively. Without thinking, I know to secure my possessions (e.g., cell phone, wallet) in crowded areas. I have chronic medical conditions and know how to keep myself safe when I am not well. I have a network of people in the city who I am able to use as resources, including medical professionals, mentors, and close friends. In New York City, I can access any place of worship and food from anywhere in the world. As a Person of Color, I know which areas will be more accepting of me and other racial and ethnic minorities. I know how to have fun without spending money (e.g., outdoor concerts, walking paths), but also know what to do when I want to splurge (e.g., off-Broadway plays, poetry readings).

In Activity 4.8, consider ways in which your identities and life experiences impact what and how you engage in social action. These experiences and identities contribute to your strengths and resources. They may also shape the lens through which you interpret and experience the world.

## ACTIVITY 4.8

### Identities and Life Experience

Think about any identities you have and knowledge areas related to your life experience (for example, if you identify as gay, you may have sought out and participated in organizations for gay communities or you may have experienced anti-gay discrimination or harassment and know what it is like to be vulnerable, and perhaps how to safeguard in particular situations).

_____

_____

_____

Think about any identities of people you are close to and knowledge areas related to their life experience (e.g., family member from different social class, partner with disability, friends who have specific life experiences that they have shared with you).

_____

_____

_____

_____

_____

_____

Reflecting on our positionality is essential when considering social action. The communities that are affected by the issues we work on are also affected by society's use of identities for privilege and oppression. One of the important aspects of coming from a privileged identity (e.g., White, economically stable, male, heterosexual, etc.) is that we may not see, or know, how an issue affects people who come from different identities than we do. For example, although we (Rebecca and Muninder) are both committed to addressing racism as a social issue, we come to it from different perspectives given our positionality and experiences of privilege and oppression. As a White woman, I (Rebecca) cannot know what it is like to be subjected to racism, so I need to know how to work on racism within White communities and how to develop solidarity with People of Color. The experience I (Muninder) have of racism is specific to being light-skinned and of Indian heritage, so I need to know how to work with individuals and communities who experience racism differently than I do, such as those who are darker-skinned, Indigenous, Latinx, or Black. Finally, it is important to consider how, as humans, we are inherently biased. Bias can be positive or negative, but there is danger because biases can be implicit, or unknown to us, and can unknowingly impact how we act toward people. We may also develop biases based on what is successful for us or known to us (e.g., religion is a helpful coping mechanism *for me, Muninder*, so I might mistakenly think having a religion is good *for everyone*) but may not be appropriate for others.

The wisdom and expertise of people who are subjected to racism is central to effectively developing and carrying out social action against racism. Further, there is a long history of White people telling People of Color what they need. If I (Rebecca) assume that I know more about how to deal with racism than a community of People of Color does, I am actually part of the problem rather than contributing to a solution. If I assume that racism is "their" problem rather than "my" problem, then I am an even bigger part of the problem. "If you have come here to help me, you are wasting your time. But if you have come because your liberation is bound up with mine, then let us work together." This quote, attributed to Lilla Watson, arose from the group she was in solidarity with. As the quote suggests, I (Rebecca) actually need to understand how racism affects me negatively and be personally invested in addressing it.

In this next activity, reflect on how you are connected to the social justice issues you are interested in working on.

### Reflection—How Are You Connected to the Issues You Care About?

Take a minute for reflection on the issues you have identified as important to you. Think about how you have described the issue in the earlier chapters and how you have come to care about those issues. Now, consider the following questions:

- How are you connected to the issue(s) you are focusing on?
- How are you affected by the issue(s) you are focusing on?
- How are you connected to others who are affected by the issue(s)?

We began this section with the goal of identifying strengths, knowledge, and resources that we each bring to social action. We also recognize that who we are adds to our work, while at the same time, it may add complexity and challenges to our involvement in different issues and with different communities.

# Areas for Growth

The main thrust of this workbook is that you have skills and knowledge that you can put to work RIGHT NOW for the issues you care about. While you are doing that good work, it is also helpful to think about your growth edges and what would be helpful for you to learn or improve upon in order to become an even better change agent. There are numerous resources shared throughout the workbook that can help you develop skills related to social action. As you read and work through the exercises, consider visiting resources such as Amnesty International's "Skill Up," which provides training modules such as cultural competency, leadership, working with media, advocacy, and action group development (https://www.amnesty.org.au/skill-up/).

In recognition of the need to identify and work on growth areas, go back through the list of skills and knowledge in Activities 4.2 and 4.3. Then, below, list those you believe would be helpful to include in your growth plan. It is not necessary to list a lot at this point; just know this is something to think about. When you read the Strategies section later in this workbook, you will find that additional areas for growth will come to mind. You can circle back and note them on this list.

**ACTIVITY 4.10**

## Areas for Growth

| Strengths | Skills | Knowledge |
|---|---|---|
| 1. | 1. | 1. |
| 2. | 2. | 2. |
| 3. | 3. | 3. |
| 4. | 4. | 4. |
| 5. | 5. | 5. |

As we transition from focusing on you and your Strengths toward focusing outward on others and your Solidarity with others, take a moment to breathe. Understand and appreciate who you are and what you bring to this endeavor. Consider ways in which you contribute or wish to contribute with others.

# chapter five

# Solidarity

 Solidarity

Solidarity, in the *Oxford Dictionary*, is defined as "Unity or agreement of feeling or action, especially among individuals with a common interest; mutual support within a group" (https://en.oxforddictionaries .com/definition/solidarity). Solidarity can be with your own community or group or can be in relation to a community outside your own. When you engage in social action related to issues in your own community, there may be an ease to solidarity because unity and trust are already present. Because I (Muninder) am a member of the Sikh community, advocating on behalf of issues that face my community often comes with some ease since I am an insider. When advocating for groups or communities where I am an outsider, such as the Black Lives Matter movement, I have to pay greater attention to ways in which power, privilege, and oppression can play out. I have to be more attentive to ways in which I do not know the lived experiences of Black community members, and I have to take my cue from them. I have to understand what their experiences are and then learn when and how to engage.

For this workbook, solidarity is really about four things:

1. honoring relationships and sustaining community;
2. respecting, supporting, and understanding others;
3. finding strength in numbers; and,
4. seeking support and camaraderie to help sustain you.

Solidarity is related to the other Ss (Strength, Strategy, and Sustainability) in that, to be effective, we need to work with others. And our relationships with others can sustain our work. In this section, we will address each of the four Solidarity areas and the challenges that sometimes come up in relationships.

## Honoring Relationships and Sustaining Community

Our relationships are vital for our roles as friend, family, and community member, and even our mental health. Relationships not only help us sustain our values, beliefs, and interests, but also help us push beyond our own interests to accomplish larger goals of serving humanity. People in our lives are often the reasons why we fight for the causes we choose.

Our social mosaic is made up of relationships, and these relationships either create community or are embedded in community. The Sikh concept of *seva*, or community service, can be helpful to understand how we create a foundation for solidarity through mutually supportive relationships. It is important to understand that mutual support does not mean equal amounts of support, and what we give is not always equivalent to what we receive. Rather, when we perceive a need, we step in to help fulfill that need. This is closer to promoting equity than equality, but more than that, it means that through serving others, we remain connected through relationships and can create and sustain community. This is distinct from helping out of pity or charity, as we understand that these interchanges are needed by everyone in a community at some time. Each interchange can be visualized as a thread that weaves people together and each interchange is essential. There is a shared responsibility by all.

The concept of seva is not about self-promotion or solely the promotion of one's own community. It is about furthering humanity and working with other communities as if they are our own. Acknowledging and honoring relationships in this way is the first step toward building solidarity.

## Respecting, Supporting, and Understanding Others

Considering our role in engaging in social action and advocacy can set a solid foundation in our approach to this work. When considering how to approach solidarity, it can be helpful to consider how liberation, allyship, political correctness, and cultural humility come up when working alongside others.

# Liberation

Liberation, or the act of freeing a person or group from oppression, is often the goal of acting in solidarity with others. Whether we are acting to promote liberty for our own community or for groups outside of our own, we need to understand that our positionality impacts how we can be in solidarity with others. We have to approach liberation in the way that Lilla Watson refers to it—that humanity is tied together and liberation and justice for one is really liberation and justice for all (quoted in Chapter 4). If we don't, we risk approaching our advocacy work from a position of above (i.e., we are above this group that is experiencing oppression, and we will save or rescue them), which rarely works well in the long run.

# Allyship

One of the central aspects of developing solidarity is allyship, or engagement in the process of building relationships and working toward justice on behalf of others in the way that an individual or community directs. Being an accomplice or partner is a good position to engage in allyship. For example, if I work toward justice in the way that I believe is best without consulting the community that experiences injustice, my actions can be oppressive, but if I engage in justice in a way that the individual or community wishes, it puts me in a position of partner supporting the other to lead. In her book *No More Heroes: Grassroots Challenges to the Savior Mentality*, Jordan Flaherty talks about the harm of "saviorism" on movements. Saviorism is where someone outside an issue who holds little knowledge of that issue imposes their vision of how to fix a problem—usually a person holding privilege, such as a White person in the case of racism. Flaherty describes how this mentality assumes that people need rescuing, and their privilege has led them to assume that they are more capable than the people who are directly affected by the issue.

# "Political Correctness"

What does it mean to be "politically correct?" It means to use labels and terms that have been deemed appropriate, often by the group with sociopolitical power. "Political correctness" is grounded in a dominant narrative of what is considered inoffensive language about groups, particularly minority groups such as those based on ethnic and racial, sexual orientation, gender, disability, religion, and other marginalized identities. It is when labels and terms are used as a surface strategy to avoid being offensive without actually understanding the meaning in context; it is largely used by people with power as a way of demonstrating that they are trying not to be offensive. In contrast, our goal in solidarity is to work from a place of respect. When we work so hard to not to offend (rather than showing respect), we prevent ourselves from a deep learning about individuals' identities, contexts, and lives and sometimes from taking responsibility for more structural oppression that we may even be a part of. Engaging in political correctness is also problematic because it elevates the dominant group's definition and labeling of other, more marginalized groups, thereby reifying power structures that keep the dominant group on top and others below.

## Cultural Humility

Our values, beliefs, and behaviors that drive us are rooted in culture. Cultural humility allows those in solidarity to approach work with community from a position of understanding that we (or our values, beliefs, and behaviors) are no more (or less) important or right than others. Our lives are very much driven by our social location, or our position in society that is influenced by our identities, histories, and contexts. Our social location influences how we may operate differently and how others may treat us differently. Cultural humility allows us to understand what is most important to others (as opposed to focusing on what is most important for us) and to work from the frame of the individual or community with whom we are advocating. Cultural humility is a way of being and a way of relating to others that is intangible but essential as a baseline for others to trust us and ultimately for effective advocacy. For example, imagine you are in a position of power or influence (e.g., know someone on the town council) and notice that unemployment is high in a neighboring community. You believe that helping increase rates of employment is important but recognize that you don't really understand the barriers or what would be most helpful in removing those barriers. This would be cultural humility. Partnering with the community members, including those who are currently seeking jobs, will be most helpful. That partnership is not the end product of cultural humility but the first step in the process. You will have to continue to work toward maintaining a stance that you are not the expert on other people's lives.

Using media produced by the groups you are building solidarity with can be a great way to learn about other communities, their strengths, and the challenges they face. For example, neither of us (Muninder or Rebecca) expects others to teach us about their communities from "scratch." We try to learn from community-based media, frame our understanding with humility and an acknowledgment of our limitations, observe and participate, and take our cues from the community. Some examples of community-based media include radio such as Latino USA and newspapers such as *Indian Country Today*. Podcasts and other digital media provide a wide range of community-generated perspectives. It is better to go to media that is generated by the community rather than the dominant media, particularly when trying to understand marginalized groups. It is important to hear the voices of people, curated by the people whose voices are to be heard rather than people outside the community. We are reminded of the very funny TED Talk by Stella Young, who talks about "inspiration porn," referring to media that uses disabled people to inspire others (https://www.ted.com/talks/stella_young_i_m_not_your_inspiration_thank_you_very_much#t-261957). She emphasizes the term *porn* because these images objectify one group of people (disabled people) to benefit other people (non-disabled people). Remember also, the voice of one person does not represent the whole group. That means that we have to be committed to hearing multiple voices of those most affected by an issue in an ongoing way.

In Activity 5.1, reflect on your experiences as an outsider and how this may impact the ways you engage with communities when working toward social justice.

## ACTIVITY 5.1

### Reaching in as an Outsider

Reflect on a time when you sought to support a community where you may have been an outsider. Consider the following questions:

1. What was your motivation for joining in solidarity?
2. How did you know what their issues were?
3. What were your issues/concerns, and how were they related to those of the community?
4. What were you willing to contribute to the community? What was your investment?
5. Was there anything you needed to give up to partner with the community?

# Strength in Numbers: Your Communities and Your Social Mosaic

One of the critical lessons of social action is that big change rarely comes from the efforts of one person. Even when one person is credited with change, it often comes in the context of a movement by larger numbers of people or communities. The kinds of problems we are trying to address require the efforts and strengths of a lot of people with different approaches to the same issue. Perhaps more importantly, no one person possesses strengths in all areas, and we cannot possibly understand issues from all viewpoints. Diversification of perspectives is essential in building a strong community and making change. For example, in the next activity, the strengths and knowledge of our friends and acquaintances enhance our efforts either through adding particular skills and resources or simply by reinforcing the ones we have. We would argue that this is the role of allies and accomplices.

In addition to the individual relationships that provide solidarity, solidarity that is based in group efforts is necessary for larger-scale change. Naomi Klein identifies organization as one of the key elements historically in large-scale social change. She talks about the challenges and limitations of putting different social issues in separate boxes—for example, climate change as one issue, discrimination as another issue, and poverty in another box. Not only is it essential to understand the interconnectedness of these issues, but when we can connect across issues, we create coalitions that are stronger.

Working together multiplies the strengths and resources available as well as amplifies the voice for any cause. It is useful to take an inventory of the people who you are connected to and with whom you maintain relationships. This is often called your network, or a social capital map. We will call it your social mosaic because it is a beautiful blend of people from different aspects of our life that are a part of who we are and who we can be. Many of us have relationships through our involvement in different types of communities, including spiritual or religious groups, social media groups, advocacy groups, parent groups, unions, workplace, professional associations, exercise groups, and our relationships with our neighbors and people we know in our community. In the following activity, think about all the relationships you have—close, distant, personal, and professional.

## ACTIVITY 5.2

### Relationships Connect Us—Your Social Mosaic

With few exceptions, humans are social beings. In the mosaic below, write in the names of the people to whom you are connected. We have created "clusters" to help you think about arenas of your life and the people within those arenas. Feel free to add clusters that seem to be missing but represent relationships in your life.

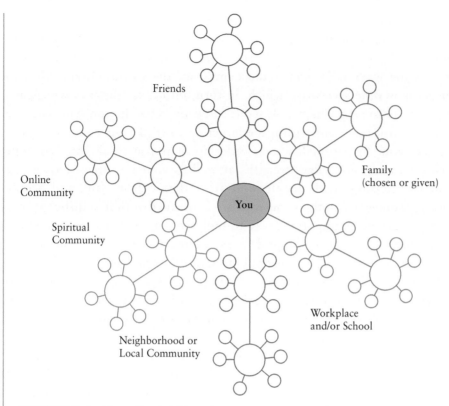

**FIGURE 5.1** Your Social Mosaic

Now reflect on the following questions as you look at your completed mosaic:

1. Are there overlaps in any areas?
2. Are there areas where you don't have many people you are connected with (for example, your neighborhood)? Would you like to develop more relationships there?
3. Are there areas where you seem to be connected to a lot of people? What do these relationships add to your life? In what ways do you contribute in those relationships?
4. Are there issues you are concerned about that others are also concerned about? Are there ways you might work with them to address the concern together?
5. How do you contribute to the well-being of people in your network? What are you able to share with them, and what is needed to sustain healthy relationships with them?

As you look back at your social mosaic, you may notice that you tend to be associated with people who are somewhat like you. Who we are and who we spend time with shapes the resources we have access to as well as the ways we perceive and experience the world. Often, this also affects how others view us, which, in turn, influences the way we engage in social action. In Chapter 4, we focused on reflecting on who you are and who you represent within the larger context of your community and society (your "positionality") in order to help you think through your relational and knowledge strengths as well as your resources. Expanding your relationships with people who are different from you, and people who are connected to the issues you are concerned with in a different way than you are, is an important way to build solidarity. There are a number of resources that can be helpful in expanding the ways to connect with others such as Southern Poverty Law Center's *Ten Ways to Fight Hate: A Community Response Guide,* which provides a range of strategies to connect with others to rise up against acts of hate (https://www.splcenter.org/20170814/ten-ways-fight-hate-community-response-guide).

Relationships are relevant in all four S-quad areas of reflection and action (Strengths, Solidarity, Strategy, and Sustainability). Our social mosaic contributes to our Strengths, including information, expertise, skills, and insights beyond those we hold ourselves. Relationships are also central for Solidarity, providing both inspiration and partners for Strategy. Solidarity and our relationships are also important for our personal and professional Sustainability, offering the comfort of human connection and acting as an important reminder of our responsibility to maintain and nurture those relationships.

## Working with Others

When people come together to work on issues they care about, there are tremendous benefits in terms of strength in numbers, camaraderie, pooling resources, creative group thinking, and others. Working together also presents challenges, even when people share passion, commitment, and goals for social change. There are some strategies and recommendations to facilitate better interpersonal communication to work together as a team. It is helpful to think about these strategies in the context of who you are, who your teammates are, and what circumstances your team is dealing with (e.g., how the group came together, what challenge the group is facing). We will focus on two aspects of teamwork: the group process and your work style.

Group process includes the way a group functions together. It can be helpful to consider how a group can work together smoothly and resolve difficulties that arise. Setting agreed-upon goals is a useful strategy when coming together as a group, and creating shared rules or agreements is essential, particularly as people come from different backgrounds and differ in values, beliefs, and behaviors. Some groups may use Robert's Rules of Order, while others have a talking stick to facilitate respectful participation. There are many strategies that are particularly helpful to facilitate difficult moments or overcoming barriers. For example, groups with insiders and outsiders may use "oops," "ouch," and "huh" as a strategy for flagging misunderstandings or microaggressions (intentional or unintentional statements or behaviors that convey assumptions, biases, and prejudices). Group agreement on as many aspects of the work is important prior to engaging in the work itself (e.g., workload), and yet this is impossible to do completely. Keeping group process in mind throughout the work will be helpful as well as members' preferences for how to work.

Work style refers to the ways you prefer to work, and knowing that helps you to work more effectively with others. In other words, there is no "one-size-fits-all" approach to working together because you bring unique needs and strengths and so do others. It is important to pay attention to your style, your strengths, and your challenges. It is also important to pay attention to how your style can play out in groups. Some things to consider can include introversion/extroversion, high-context/low-context communication, and formal/informal communication. For example, extroverts get energy from being around others, while introverts recharge by being alone; we generally have both extroversion and introversion but to varying degrees. When working with others, this can cause challenges if some individuals want to constantly meet, while others want to work completely alone. However, having both extroverts and introverts can be helpful when working with groups; we just have to respect that our work styles are different and equally valuable.

# Finding Support and Camaraderie to Sustain You

When we are engaged in advocacy or social action, being connected with others who join together with us can also sustain us. The potential is there because we are working together with at least one shared value and purpose.

EXAMPLE

### Rebecca

I was jolted to start participating in breast cancer fundraising walks about fifteen years ago when my cousin was taken by the disease. I had never done anything like that before but signed up, reached out to family and friends for pledges of donations, then arrived to see thousands of people (mostly women) in all variations of pink, clever signs, hats, and boisterous teams. I had not invited anyone to come with me, and honestly, it never occurred to me to do so, perhaps because this was my way of honoring and mourning the loss of my cousin. Although I felt alone, the organizers and other walkers were very welcoming. It was very moving to be a part of a surge of excited and determined people working toward a central goal. Throughout the walk, various people would stride alongside me and strike up a conversation. Often, they would start with, "Are you walking alone?" Initially I responded by saying "yes," but as the day wore on, I realized that I didn't feel alone. I changed my response: "No, I'm walking with 5,000 other people." This walk has allowed me to engage in seva along with others who have either directly or indirectly been impacted by cancer. And this seva came from community but also created community by the act of doing for others and doing for something larger than the self. The walk was never easy in the sense that I had blisters by the end and my feet hurt, but I found the support to keep going, and maybe I provided it, too.

In a podcast interview, DeRay McKesson (2015) talked about the importance of solidarity in his experiences in Ferguson, Missouri, after the Michael Brown killing.

> I think so often in the beginning, we didn't know each other's names but we knew each other's hearts. There were people that I trusted my life with that I've never seen again, I don't know anything about them. But we hopped the three fences, to get to the whatever … it was the beginning of a new community (https://soundcloud.com/thecombatjackshow/the-deray-mckesson-episode).

He continued to say how inspiring it was to be in a community of people in Ferguson. The interviewer asked, "How alone did you feel when you went out there?" McKesson responded,

> I didn't at all, I had no friends, I literally didn't know anybody. But there was so much beauty in Blackness. I'll never forget the

woman who brought out her grill every day and made hot dogs and hamburgers on the corner, and you're like, "yesss," and there was so much water. You're like drowning in water. Everyone had water, pizza, there was REAL community out there.

When we go into these acts of advocacy and work toward social justice, the support and camaraderie of others can sustain our work and add momentum to further the cause. Moreover, sometimes building support and camaraderie *is* social action.

## Solidarity as Social Action

In and of itself, being in solidarity with others can be social advocacy and action. When I (Muninder) consider ways in which friends from outside the Sikh community engage in solidarity with me, I can identify a range of involvement. Some have signed up for news alerts from Sikh organizations and educated others, while others have stood up against oppression that a Sikh individual or group has faced and have attended organized marches. A number of positions and strategies we take can foster solidarity, including that of accomplice, legal observer, witness, and accompaniment. When we are outsiders, a crucial aspect that defines these actions as solidarity is the extent to which we do them as directed by, or in partnership with, individuals and communities, as opposed to acting from our own frame of reference. We will discuss these as strategies in more depth later in the next chapter.

# chapter six

# Strategy and Real Action

*Big Picture, Playbook, and Everyday Action*

Strategy

One of the reasons people become overwhelmed is that many of the issues that they care about are really big, often with many systems and people involved at all levels of government and society. At the same time, there are individual efforts that can be helpful each day. One of the challenges is that change is often slow, and we don't always know the outcome of our efforts.

Strength and Solidarity are about understanding the power that you have. Strategy, as an area of reflection, is designed to help you think about how you can use that power by tapping into guidance from decades, even centuries, of people who have taken action. It may be helpful to think about strategies in terms of how big the scope is: in other words, how complex the issues are and how much time and effort is required to take the action needed. We think it might to helpful to think about three aspects of strategy: *Big Picture*, *Playbook*, and *Everyday Action*. The *Big Picture* is the vision for a positive future and an understanding of what may need to be different or what might need to change to make that a reality. Really big changes are complex, and actions must extend over time. Making this happen requires smaller long-term and short-term strategic actions (the *Playbook*), as well as really immediate individual and singular actions (*Everyday Action*).

Strategy, as an area for reflection for social action, is designed to help you consider different approaches and access a wealth of resources and wisdom that can help your efforts. The following activities are designed to help you practice different types of actions and determine which strategies might make the most sense given your strengths, focus, and the situation or problem. An important caveat we mentioned at the beginning of the book is particularly relevant here: strategies do not have to be linear, and readers may find some parts of the workbook more relevant than others for them. Take what is useful, leave what doesn't fit, but also reflect on what the lack of fit is about. Is it simply not appropriate for the situation? Are you missing some skills or information to use that strategy? Or does it just feel outside your comfort zone?

## The *Big Picture*: A Vision for a Positive Future

The *Big Picture* is just what it sounds like: the big vision of the way things could look if the issue is no longer an issue, as well as the broad path of how to get there. As described at the beginning of this workbook, it is helpful to have a vision for a positive future. We are reminded of the movie *The Black Panther* and the positive reaction to the homeland of Wakanda (e.g., pride, hopefulness, validation) of many of our friends, particularly People of Color. There are many reasons why the movie is such a cultural phenomenon, one of which is that it presents a vision of what life could be like in Africa if colonization, oppression, and slavery had not existed. It is important to have a vision to guide action. A vision without action is a fantasy, but vision *with* action is a powerful force.

Because many of the issues we face in the world today are big and may require long-range planning and many players, the vision of the *Big Picture* can help you to stay the course even in times when you may feel discouraged, distracted, and overwhelmed. Systemic change is often a complex process requiring significant groundwork and coordination. The big picture makes sure your efforts are going in a positive direction toward making real and significant change. It can also help you keep your "eyes on the prize" and remember how your daily actions contribute to this big change. Fortunately, YOU ARE NOT ALONE. You are a part of the big picture, and whole communities are working toward the same thing. In fact, if you are working on it alone, there is a problem.

The big picture can also help to begin to shift your vision into action by examining where you may begin working. In a 2015 podcast interview, in regard to different phases within movements addressing police violence in Black communities, DeRay McKesson said:

In the beginning, we were trying to convince people that there was a problem and exposing the problem. Now we are getting to a point where we are trying to solve the problem and the reality is that the strategy for those two things will be different. We won't undo 400 years of oppression in 300 days, that is an unrealistic expectation. In this moment, I think about the phases, we were fighting, then community building, and now we are in what I call this phase of preparing to win. It is this moment where we are stepping back and saying what does the win look like. (https://soundcloud.com/thecombatjackshow/the-deray-mckesson-episode)

In this next activity, you will reflect on your vision of a positive future. Then, we will ask you to think about the barriers currently in place that make that positive future more difficult to achieve. The work you have done to engage in solidarity can help you here. What have you learned by reaching out to people who also care about these issues—people who have a similar vision? To move toward action, it may be helpful in the big picture to think about the issue and barriers at three levels: societal, community or organizational, and individual. In other words, the issue or barriers may be something that is widespread across the world, your country, or your state. You may find the issue or barriers in your local community, your place of work, or your school. You may also find them in the individuals you interact with, family, neighbors, or coworkers. In the *Playbook* section, we will talk about a variety of concrete strategies that can be used in those three realms: society, locally, and individually.

## ACTIVITY 6.1

### Vision for a Positive Future Through Collage

**What you will need:** A sheet of paper at least 8.5" × 11" (used paper is fine), scissors, glue stick or tape, magazines, photos, newspapers, or anything with images. You can also do this activity electronically (e.g., digital images) if that is a more comfortable medium.

#### Part 1: How do things look to you now?

For one side of the paper, choose images that represent how you see your world now. They could represent your job, your life, your family, your community, as well as the challenges and injustices you see. Gather the images into a pile until you find enough to represent the most important aspects. If you don't find the right images or words, you can write in words by hand.

Then, cut, arrange, and glue the images and words into place.

**Part 2: What's your vision for the future?**

For the other side of the paper, choose images that represent aspects of the future you would like to see, for example, images that express the way you hope your community, family, job, and the world will look. Cut, arrange, and glue the images and words into place.

**Reflection questions:**

- What differences do you see between the world now and your vision for the future?
- Did you have trouble finding images for the collages? Is it possible that the types of magazines and newspapers you have are somewhat limited in their scope (e.g., not very diverse)? If you did the activity electronically, how did you search for images, and is it possible that your search history limited the images that appeared? How do the media sources you use shape or reflect the lens through which you see the world? What would it mean to branch out beyond the news sources and media you currently have access to?
- How can you contribute to making your vision a reality?

We hope you use this last question as a touchstone, or anchor, as you work through the rest of the book.

As we talk about the *Playbook* and *Everyday Actions*, we will give examples of some of the actions we, Muninder and Rebecca, have chosen to take. We do this simply as examples of some of the ways we have tried to work toward our visions, and not as the right or perfect way to go, but in the hopes of being a bit more concrete. It is important to emphasize that there is rarely one right or perfect action, and often action does not result in immediate resolution of big systemic issues. All kinds of actions are needed by all kinds of people, persistently over time. You are an important part of that movement.

## The *Playbook*: Starting with the Basics

The *Playbook* includes concrete strategies that contribute to the *Big Picture*. There are many different approaches for addressing a concern or problem, each with its benefits and challenges. In fact, most big problems require many different kinds of people working on many different kinds of approaches. For example, following the killing of seventeen high school students in Parkland, Florida, in February 2018, the United States witnessed an increased visibility of voices and marches calling attention to gun violence. Yet, there have been many people pressing this issue for quite some time in various ways without the same visibility. For example, the Brady Campaign to Prevent Gun Violence has been working for decades to secure and maintain progress on legislation to reduce gun violence by enforcing background checks, improving communication about dangerous histories of individuals wanting to purchase guns, and more recently, influence of the gun lobbies, such as the National Rifle Association (NRA) on presidential elections and legislative decisions. A more thorough description can be found in the actual Brady Bill (www.bradycampaign.org/timeline-of-the-brady-bills-passage). Our Destiny STL is a youth-led organization formed after the killing of Michael Brown (Ferguson, Missouri, August 2014) to address gun violence and profiling of Black individuals by the police (https://www.unitedway.org/shining-a-light/the-concert/our-destiny-stl). The organization focuses on community outreach, youth leadership, youth voter registration drives, organizing demonstrations, and forming relationships between the police department and the community. The American Psychological Association, among other health-related professional associations, has taken positions against gun violence and contributed research findings to support policies and legislation (http://www.apa.org/advocacy/gun-violence/index.aspx). These three examples illustrate the range of many different types of action being taken by politicians, community members, professionals, and youth for national-level and community-level change with strategies including policy and legislation, increasing awareness of a problem through media and organizing, community building, creating dialogue and cooperation between community and police, and empowerment of groups affected by the issue. Tod Sloan, a friend and critical psychologist who blogged about systemic change and the relationship to his own health challenges prior to his passing in December 2018, wrote:

> In the activist world, people can have several different strategies and goals. Each has its place ... The first is to try to stop bad things that are happening (like torture or pollution). The second is to raise awareness of problems so people will change their practices accordingly. The third is to "prefigure" the changes we hope to see by constructing spaces, communities, practices that demonstrate better ways of living together and meeting our needs. (https://todsloan.tumblr.com/post/174950229342/life-strategies)

To reiterate the point, any big change needs lots of different people with different expertise and wisdom to tackle the issues from many different angles. So, where do you fit? The answer to this question can flow from your vision, focus, and goals. Additionally, the specific strategies you select are hopefully chosen to maximize your strengths and appropriateness to situation; moreover, the benefits should outweigh the costs. In choosing the right strategies, and your place in them, you should consider the issue, the wisdom of the community affected by the issue, your ability to carry out the strategy (your strengths), and the possible outcomes and consequences of each action. The flowchart below reflects a process you can use to build a playbook and decide on strategies for your social action goals. Once you implement the strategy, a critical step is to reflect on how well your actions addressed the goal or problem. If it worked well or helped make progress toward larger system change, then it may be a good strategy to continue. If not, then it may be time to revisit potential alternative strategies and try a different approach.

In this chapter, we will give a brief introduction to a number of different strategies and provide you with resources on "how to" for each of the strategies. Then, we present some activities to help you evaluate the different possible paths you might consider for your social action plan, including the benefits and costs you might encounter. One of the things we have learned is that sometimes jumping to action is helpful; other times, the costs outweigh the benefits. Some of us already have a good sense of strategy and have had experience in a wide range of social

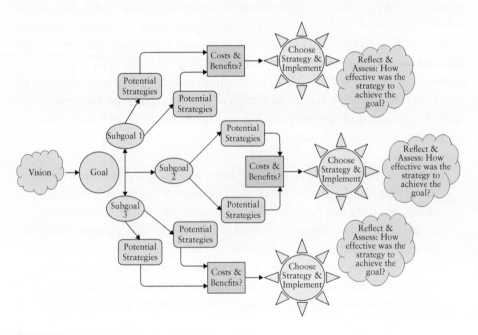

**FIGURE 6.1** Strategy flowchart

action. Examining costs and benefits may seem redundant or may help us look at options we hadn't considered before. For those of us who are still shaping our social action identities, this process can be helpful, especially if we talk and listen to people who have experienced costs and benefits firsthand.

# Getting Started: Understanding the Issue

Before talking strategy, it is helpful to reflect on some important aspects of the issues or problems you hope to address. In this activity, you will identify and seek to more deeply understand your social justice issue of concern.

## ACTIVITY 6.2

### Understanding the Issue — Assessing the Situation

Think about the issues you want to focus on. Your responses to the following questions can help you determine some approaches to start with and strategies that make the most sense given the issue and what you have to contribute in terms of knowledge, skills, relationships, positionality, and passion. If you have trouble, look at the example below and then come back and try to answer the questions for one of your issues. These questions may take some time because they ask you to really investigate the issue. If, at first glance, you are not able to answer all of these, plan some time to do your homework and fill it out step by step.

1. What is the issue or concern (e.g., sexism in your workplace, police violence against communities of color, inadequate health care for seniors, harassment of immigrants, separation of families seeking asylum), and what are the different aspects of this issue?
   a. Who is affected negatively and in what ways?
   b. How are you connected to this issue? (positionality)
   c. Is this a national concern, statewide, local, and/or organizational?
2. Who is already working on this issue? What is already being done?
   a. Identify and describe allies (who else cares about this issue?) and resources.
   b. Is there anyone who might oppose change or social action?
   c. What, if anything, is already being done to address this issue?
3. Who has power in this issue?
   a. What systems are involved (particular offices, policies, etc.)?
   b. Who has decision-making power or influence?
   c. What do you want to change or have an impact on?

In the following example, I (Rebecca) explore these questions as they relate to the desecration of Indigenous sacred land in the San Francisco Bay Area.

**EXAMPLE**

### Desecration of Indigenous Land

1.  What is the issue or concern? *There is a history of theft of Indigenous land in the United States, broken treaties, and disrespect of sacred ancestral lands. In the San Francisco Bay Area, a heavily populated and developed metropolitan region, the Ohlone people are the original peoples of the land prior to settlement by Spanish and then U.S. settlers. There continues to be development of land that has sacred ancestral meaning for the Ohlone people.*

    a.  Who is affected negatively, and in what ways? *This is a big question with complex responses. Briefly, Ohlone and other Indigenous people who reside in the Bay Area as well as nationally are affected due to the repeated loss of sacred land. The residents of the Bay Area are also affected in that the richness of the original peoples and the members of the community currently are being relegated to history. Sacred, important, and beautiful land is being developed into shopping malls, parking lots, and condos.*

    b.  How are you connected to this issue? (positionality) *As a White person, I feel affected because this development is one more example of colonization and betrayal of the Indigenous community here by people who look like me. I am a settler in this land, and I feel angry and sad that by being here, I contribute to the loss of Indigenous communities here. This is even worse when sacred land is developed for profit. It is important to note that I am not part of the Ohlone community or any Indigenous community. My positionality is as an outsider, someone who cares but is relatively new to involvement in this specific local issue. I do know one of the central leaders in the local movement because of her generosity in speaking to a professional group I belong to.*

    c.  Is this a national concern, statewide, local, or organizational? *Desecration of sacred Indigenous land is a national concern, statewide, and local issue. In the Bay Area, there are specific actions that I can focus on. For this example, I will focus on action that I can take locally. There is one specific area, the West Berkeley Shellmounds, within Berkeley, California, that is currently under review for development.*

2. Who is already working on this issue? What is already being done? *There is one central organization that is working to address and intervene in the development of the West Berkeley Shellmounds, Indian People Organizing for Change (IPOC), along with three Ohlone family bands (http://ipocshellmoundwalk.homestead.com). Sogorea Te Land Trust is a related organization that was created to reclaim land (and rematriation) in order to reestablish sacred areas for gathering and ceremony* (https://www.sfchronicle.com/bayarea/article/Indigenous-women-lead-effort-to-reclaim-ancestral-12384730.php).

   a. Identify and describe allies (who else cares about this issue?) and resources. *There are several organizations that are supporting the effort in addition to the leaders. One organization, Showing Up for Racial Justice (SURJ)* (https://www.surjbayarea.org), *is a national network of local groups organizing White people for social change. The Bay Area chapter has been active supporting the efforts around preservation of the West Berkeley Shellmounds and taking direction from IPOC. Cultural Conservancy is another organization that works to support Indigenous communities in the Bay Area* (http://www.nativeland.org).

   b. What, if anything, is already being done to address this issue? *There have been numerous efforts led by Indigenous leaders to halt the development process and propose an alternative that would recognize, honor, and teach about the sacred Shellmound area* (https://www.sfchronicle.com/bayarea/article/Indigenous-women-lead-effort-to-reclaim-ancestral-12384730.php). *These efforts have included testifying at city council meetings, letter writing campaigns to city planning commissions, rallies at the site, educational sessions, and other events.*

3. Who has power in this issue? *There are multiple groups that have different types of power in this situation, including the developers, the city council, development agencies, Sogorea Te Land Trust, and others.*

   a. What systems are involved (particular offices, policies, etc.)? *The City of Berkeley–Berkeley Zoning Adjustment Board.*

   b. Who has decision-making power or influence? *At different points in time depending on the approval process, different offices may have decision-making power. Leaders in Sogorea Te Land Trust are the best source of information on knowing who has the decision-making power for each part of the bureaucratic process.*

4. What do you want to try to change or have an impact on? *I would like to support efforts to preserve that land as one small contribution to the larger issue of preserving Indigenous land locally.*

Breaking each of these components down in the activity, reflecting on them, and taking a look at different aspects that I (Rebecca) might not be aware of helps me to make sure I understand the context in which this issue, and previous action, has taken place. It also helps me to honor the work that others, especially those in the community, have been doing and how I can be most helpful. In the example provided, I had heard about this issue and participated in some events, but I gained a much deeper understanding of the organization and efforts to address this issue during an event where I met Corrina Gould, a Chochenyo and Karkin Ohlone leader from the Confederated Villages of Lisjan/Ohlone and the cofounder and lead organizer for IPOC. The more events I attended, the more I learned about accomplices (people and organizations that supported the efforts through research, education, fundraising, and bringing additional people to the cause). Learning all of this also helped me to understand ways that I might be most helpful and contribute to organized efforts already taking place, rather than initiating efforts on my own which likely would be less productive and, in fact, may actually demonstrate a lack of respect for those working long before I became involved.

The above activity is one of the most important for people who are new to social action. For people who are already involved in activism, it can also be a way of stepping back and reflecting on the work, understanding how others might be involved, and making decisions about strategies and actions. This type of reflection also helps to uncover areas where more information would be helpful, who is missing from the picture, and who can help find concrete information about the impact of this issue or the potential of change.

The reflection on who is already involved also helps to strengthen and deepen your understanding and how you communicate the issue to others. The following activity provides an opportunity to revisit your elevator speech and add more information (or identify missing information) to help take you to the next step. As you work on this elevator speech, consider who your audience might be and how they might hear your message.

## ACTIVITY 6.3

### Solidifying the Foundation of Your Elevator Speech

For this activity, you will need to go back to the elevator speech that you started in Chapter 2. Reflect on what you wrote for Activity 2.7, where you created the beginning of your elevator speech (#1 and part of #2), and then build on that.

1. *Introduce yourself, position, and place (look back at Activity 2.7).*

2. *What is the issue, and why is it important? (In Activity, 2.7, you looked at why it is important to you personally; here we want you to think more broadly. Why is the issue important beyond yourself?)*

- Think about what you learned in the process you used to examine your issue in Activity 6.2 ("Understanding the Issue"). What compelling stories or statistics can be helpful in catching the listener's interest? Personal stories about people who are deeply affected by the issue, combined with statistics that show that it is not just one person or one family, make the issue emotionally and rationally compelling.
- Now, in two or three sentences, state your issue and why it is important.

### *Example:*

"Forced family separation and deportation results in long-term trauma for children. Maria, a five-year-old, lies limp surrounded by hundreds of other children in a detention center near the U.S.-Mexico border. About 2,300 children have been taken from their families by U.S. Immigration and Customs officials; most of the families were trying to seek asylum in the United States from violence in their home country. These families are not only being torn apart, but they are also being prevented from seeking asylum." (The information contained in this example was taken from articles in the American Psychological Association's *Monitor* [https://www.apa.org/news/apa/2018/border-family-separation.aspx] and an article in the *New York Times* [https://www.nytimes.com/2018/06/18/health/migrant-children-mental-health.html]).

Once you have figured out who is already involved in action and how they are involved, you can start thinking about ways you can contribute, and which strategies you might participate in or initiate. There are all kinds of actions that can be taken and multiple levels where your efforts can be focused. In the following sections, we provide some basic guidance to help you get started. We also provide resources so you can go further in taking action and develop your skills and knowledge.

# Approach to Strategy

Reading about social and political movements and the experiences of people within those movements provides us with a wealth of insight for approaching large-scale change. What we find is that there is no one singular approach that is the "right" way to do things. However, there are many lessons about how to consider possible strategies, different approaches that might fit the situation, and how they might fit with you as a person engaging in action. Some of what distinguishes different strategies are their philosophies about how change occurs, the role of change, the place of participatory engagement in leadership and determination, and cultural and religious teachings. Our choices about strategies are also influenced by the lessons we learn from our loved ones and those who have already worked to help bring about change.

We have organized playbook strategies into the following sections: communicating with legislators and policy makers; working with groups; communicating with media; and, communicating with the public. Within each of these, you can be a leader, a team member, or a supporter. Some strategies look like quiet action aimed at consistent gradual change, whereas others look loud, demanding immediate action. Movements are made of poets, strategists, revolutionaries, parents, students, elders, children, musicians, educators, mechanics, tech workers, artists, cooks, marketing professionals, introverts, extroverts—and the list goes on and on. Basically, social change comes from the involvement of all kinds of people who push for change in all kinds of ways. Whether you believe in a "gradualist" approach or a "revolutionary" approach, there are strategies that can help make your work more effective.

It is important to note that many of the strategies described in this workbook can be focused on the global or national level, state level, local level, or even your own organization or neighborhood. As you read through them, consider the context that you are focusing on and how these strategies might fit with that context. For example, if you are considering ways that you may work within your job, organization, or school, some strategies may have clear applications, while others may be more clearly focused in politics.

There are a few basic principles that apply to many of the strategies discussed in this chapter:

- Know your issue—Learn what you can about the issue, different sides of the issue, and a little basic history about the issue. You don't need to know everything about it but gather some basic facts and then fact check to confirm your arguments are on more solid ground. Presumably, you will learn a lot about your issue along the way.

- Know your audience—Whether you are planning to talk with friends or family, inform the public, motivate others to care about your issue, or try to persuade or inform policy makers and decision makers, it is helpful to know to whom you are talking, what they believe about the issue, and what they already know (or think they know) about your issue. Are they in support, opposed, or neutral? Have they already taken action? Know who has what kind of power to make or promote change on this issue. Will they be more convinced from a rational perspective or emotional perspective?

- Focus your message—One of the challenges is to stay on point when there are so many issues we feel passionate about. In most cases, even though many issues are important, if we combine too many issues or concerns, your audience will lose focus and will be less likely to hear your message clearly. Decide which issue and message you are going to carry, then stick with that. Decide what the "hook" will be (what will get them interested enough to hear you out), a brief set of talking points or information that are the basics of what you would like them to know, and, finally, what you want or need from them (e.g., action, commitment, voting, etc.).

Your elevator speech allows you to summarize your message about one particular topic and strategy. You will want to adapt your elevator speech slightly to connect with different audiences and what they might find most relevant and compelling. The strategies discussed throughout the rest of this chapter vary in many ways, the most important of which is the audience. Whom does the strategy target? Legislators? Decision makers? The media? The public? Other activists? In Activity 6.4, note your initial thoughts about strategies to engage in social action.

## ACTIVITY 6.4

### Your First Thoughts About Action

In the first few chapters of the workbook, you articulated the central issues you plan to focus on. Now, what strategies come to mind?

- Are there strategies the community is already using?
- If so, is there a way you may support those efforts?
- Who might be the focus of your energy if you are going to reach out to others who are not engaged in this issue?
- What would be compelling to them?
- What might your role be, and which skills or knowledge might be useful?

You can approach this chapter in a variety of ways, depending on your needs and style. For example, it may be helpful to read through all of the strategies so you become familiar with a wide range of different types of approaches. Or you may choose to jump around and read about strategies you are less familiar with. Regardless of how you approach this chapter, we encourage you to consider using this as a tool to expand your comfort zone and broaden your repertoire of possible approaches you can take. At the end of this chapter, after presenting the range of different types of strategies, we will invite you to consider some questions to help you assess which strategy might be most appropriate given the situation, the possible consequences of a strategy, and your goals.

## Communicating and Working with Legislators, Government, and Policy Makers

One of the ways to call attention to an issue is to consider legislation or policies that either make the issue worse or have the potential to improve things. You may already be familiar with how legislation works, and if so, you can skim the next page or two as we give a brief description of the basics.

Legislation typically refers to state or national level laws or proposed laws, whereas policies refer to a set of rules. Procedures and practices refer to how things are done, one being more formal and the other being less formal. All of these can impact an issue or community. For example, with the issue of gun violence, there are federal and state laws that dictate the age at which someone can legally purchase a gun and what types of guns can be sold. There are also state and federal laws that spell out the procedures for gun sales, including how the sale of guns should happen (e.g., whether the buyer must be competent to use a gun safely, whether the buyer must provide proof of identity, whether there are any background checks about the buyer's history of violence, and how long they should wait after requesting to buy a gun to receive the gun).

There are legislators in every state that determine state laws, including the governor, the state senate, and state assembly. Each of these bodies are elected by constituents; in other words, voters in their state, county, or district. Contacting your legislators and making your voice heard is important regardless of whether your legislator agrees with your position or not. If their actions and opinions are opposite from yours, they need to hear from you (and as many other people as possible) to know the opinion of their voters. If they are in agreement with your position, it is also helpful for them to hear from you whether it is a thank you, an affirmation that they have your support, or to provide them with additional information and data that can help them fight for that issue.

An example of individuals and communities working together with government officials is ThriveNYC, an initiative of the New York City mayor's office in response to the local and national mental health crisis. One component that has made this initiative unique is the intentional involvement of cultural and religious communities in the city. The mayor's office works with mosques, synagogues, gurdwaras, and churches around the city and their religious leaders. This allows a bidirectional flow of information, whereby policies and procedures can be localized to address issues that are unique to each community. I (Muninder) sat on a panel with other Sikh scholars and practitioners and the deputy mayor to inform the Sikh community of the mental health challenges we face, how mental health services can be accessed, and the ways in which mental health services can be used to supplement Sikh ways of healing. Simultaneously, we informed the mayor's office about unique stressors and barriers to mental health care access for the Sikh community, such as Islamophobia, hate crimes, and threats based on immigration status.

## Emails, Phone Calls, and Postcards

A quick and easy way of contacting your legislators, whether state or federal, is through the written or spoken word. You can communicate your feelings or wishes in a succinct way that can be very effective if you use specific guidelines: state your issue and your position on it; stay focused on your message; customize your message; include how the issue affects you, your community, or your family directly; offer a compelling story; and, most importantly, state what you want your legislator to do about it. This method is also relevant for *Everyday Actions* because these are really easy, singular actions that take little time. Activity 6.5 prompts you to practice engagement in one action.

### ACTIVITY 6.5

#### One Email, One Phone Call

This activity has two parts: choosing your issue, then drafting an email or making a phone call.

**Part 1:** Choose one of your central priority issues or one of your everyday action issues.

The following resources can help you find a specific decision, legislation, or event to narrow the focus of your message and can even provide you with some language to use. In addition to these resources, you can also go directly to an advocacy group that is already working on the issue to find specific actionable items. Some tips: your letter or call has more power if you are a constituent and/or if you can write a legislator who is involved in a committee who has decision-making power; and your message is clear about what action you want taken. Possible action may be continued advocacy on an issue (if they are in favor of your position), voting a particular way, or even providing you with information about a bill whose status is unclear (some bills are referred back to committee, and it is unclear whether they are still being considered).

***Examples of resources specific to the United States:***

***Congress.Gov*** (https://www.congress.gov) is a federal website that informs you about legislation (current and past), which committees are involved in specific decisions and bills, and how your representatives have voted in past legislation. You can look up legislation using a keyword, and it will provide you with any specific legislation being considered or proposed, the name of the bill, the sponsors of the bill, the committees involved, and the status of the bill.

***GovTrack*** (https://www.govtrack.us) is a project of Civic Impulse LLC, an independent organization that provides an easy way to find out what legislation might be pending regarding issues you are concerned about. It also provides you with the contact information for your senators and representatives. You can sign up to receive action alerts regarding issues of interest.

***5 Calls*** (https://5calls.org) is an independent web tool (nonprofit) that was created to make it easy to identify issues and call your legislators and make your voice heard. On their main web page, if you provide your zip code, the web tool provides a list different current issues you can prioritize. Once you have indicated interest in an issue, the tool will provide possible actions to address the issue. These may include specific legislation or petitioning regarding a specific issue or politician. When you identify an issue, the site provides you with a script that you can use regarding the issue.

**Part 2:** Now that you have narrowed your focus for this activity, plan out what you will say. Then draft the email and/or draft a script for one phone call to at least one of your legislative representatives. We have provided you with a sample letter template to use, if you wish.

***Example of a letter:***

"Dear (<u>name of legislator or decision maker</u>),

I am (<u>a constituent, concerned community member</u>) writing to express my concern about (<u>issue</u>). This is important to me (or my community) because (summarize in two or three sentences the reasons it is important to you, what you think the impact is, etc.; it helps to use a personal story or example). I am asking for (Senator, Representative, whomever you are calling) to vote (or advocate) for (your position; it helps if you can list a specific legislation or bill). This issue is of critical importance and I appreciate the (legislator's name) action on this."

Notes: You may want to adjust this script, depending on whether the legislator is opposed, neutral, or supportive of your position. If you are a constituent, it is helpful to provide your zip code or district. If you are calling, you will most likely be connected to a staff member or voicemail.

Scheduling a day and time weekly that you will call one of your representatives is one way to help follow through on your good intentions. If you feel anxious about doing it, Cordelia, in her comicblog, *Echo through the Fog*, provides an amusing illustrated guide on "how to call your representative when you have social anxiety" (http://echothroughthefog.cordeliadillon.com/post/153393286626/how-to-call-your-reps-when-you-have-social-anxiety).

## In-Person Visits

Visits to your legislators or other public officials can be very effective ways of communicating your concern, sharing information, and developing ongoing relationships with decision makers and their staff. There are a number of things that can help you have the biggest impact:

- Know the right people to talk to;
- Know their schedules;
- Know what issues they are working on and what committees they serve on;
- Know their position on issues;
- Develop a relationship with them; and
- Be prepared for the visit; even something as little as wearing clothing that aligns with their office dress code can make a difference.

As with the other strategies discussed above, when planning a visit, prepare yourself by narrowing down the issue you wish to discuss. Create your list of talking points: what is the issue, and why is it an issue? Whom does it affect, and how? What action do you want to see the legislator take? Be sure to include any data or compelling stories that can make an impact on the legislator or their staff member as well as a reiteration of the action you'd like to see.

As we said earlier, you can have the most impact on legislators when you are a part of their constituency and they are supposed to represent you and your district. Elected officials typically have offices in their local district as well as in Washington, DC (for federal legislators), or in the state capital (for state legislators). The website of the legislator should provide you with information regarding which office they will be in during a specified time as well as what issues, bills, committees, and voting record they have as it relates to your concern. The Indivisible Guide (https://www.indivisible.org/guide/advocacy-tactics/district-office-visits/) is written by former congressional staffers and provides great insider information and tips. Some of the recommendations they give include scheduling your visit when the legislator will be in that office; be prepared with your points and questions and insist on meeting with the legislator directly. If you are aiming to meet with a member of Congress or a senator, it is most likely that even if you have arranged to meet with the legislator directly, you may be meeting with one of their staff members. If you are meeting with a state politician, you may be more likely to meet with the elected official directly. It is important that you treat the staff member with the same level of respect that you would give to the elected official, and use the opportunity to share your message and data. They are the representative of the elected leader and their ability (and likelihood) of emphasizing your message powerfully to the legislator depends on the clarity and power of your message. At the end of the meeting, make sure you reiterate the action you want the legislator to take and that you would like them to follow up with you. Leave a brief, written summary of what you shared with them, what action you want, and contact information for follow-up. If the staff or legislator asks a question you are unable to answer, be honest and let them know you will look into it and get back to them. This also gives you an opportunity to follow up with them and continue to develop a relationship.

One additional recommendation from the Indivisible Guide is to arrange to visit the legislator as a group if possible because "It is much harder for district or DC staff to turn away a group than a single constituent, even without an appointment." In addition, use social media to communicate what you have done, take photos (with permission, of course), and share your message broadly, including the response of the legislator or their staffer.

Finally, consider identifying a legislator and office to develop ongoing relationships with based on the issues you care about or that their constituency cares about. When the staff or legislator becomes familiar with you, the issues you care about, and your ability to bring compelling information, stories or people to them, they are more likely to call on you in the future. In this next activity, you will broaden and build on the previous activity.

**ACTIVITY 6.6**

## Laying the Groundwork for an In-Person Visit

You can use this activity to build on the email/phone activity by using the same issue. Follow each of the steps, writing in as much information as you can gather. The resources listed in Activity 6.5 as well as the website of the decision maker are useful here as well.

1. Background

   - Issue:
   - Decision maker or legislator and key staff member:
   - When are they in the office? What committees do they serve on? What is their voting record or position on your issue?

2. Talking Points

   - Why is it an issue?
   - Why is this issue important?
   - Whom does it affect, and how?
   - Do you have a personal story, research, or some expertise you can include here?
   - What action do you want to see the legislator take?
   - What would you like in the form of follow-up? (This can include actions and timing.)

# Taking Action Through Advocacy Organizations

Probably the easiest way to take action is to get involved with advocacy organizations that focus on issues you care about. Some advocacy organizations focus their work on specific issues (e.g., United We Dream, Southern Poverty Law Center, Showing Up for Racial Justice), while others focus more broadly (e.g., Alliance for Justice, Indivisible). Typically, an advocacy organization aims to raise awareness about an issue both for the public and decision makers such as legislators, policy makers, judicial systems, and organizations as well as encourage action. They do this through public information campaigns, mobilizing committed members, organizing public events such as demonstrations, rallies, boycotts, raising funds for legal defense of individuals affected by the issue, and other activities. Taking action through advocacy organizations has many benefits, including built-in structure and momentum, solidarity with others who are committed to similar issues, pooling of resources and expertise, tracking urgent developments, and more. In addition, some advocacy organizations provide training to expand your knowledge about the issue as well as develop skills and strategies for taking action. Over the past several years, the use of social media and digital communication has allowed advocacy organizations and concerned community members to communicate and mobilize very rapidly. Some organizations will send out alerts to subscribers with updates and information about how to participate in rallies or events supporting or opposing a situation or decision.

In addition to advocacy organizations available to the general public, professional associations and unions for specific disciplines or occupations often function as advocacy organizations. Typically, the primary advocacy focus of professional associations is to further their own profession, organize events and opportunities for networking, as well as lobby on behalf of the organization, its members, and the profession as a whole. However, professional associations may also advocate on issues that affect individuals and communities who are served by members of the profession. For example, the American Psychological Association (APA) has multiple offices that focus on issues and communities served by psychologists. The Public Interest Directorate of APA is one such office that focuses on issues such as poverty, aging, etc. Similar to professional associations, unions can also function as advocacy organizations. Unions are also related to specific occupations or employment sectors and focus on advocacy, mostly around issues related to its members including negotiating contracts for its members, advocating for individual members but also may serve as an organizing force to support or oppose public policies or legislative decisions such as funding of public education. Some unions also sponsor bills and/or take stands on social issues and provide avenues for members to take action. For example, the California Faculty Association sponsored a bill in the California State Legislature to amend the legal standard of police use of deadly force. Professional associations and unions may also have government relations offices or staff whose job is to develop and maintain relationships with legislators and policy makers.

In the next activity, you will identify different types of organizations that are working on social justice issues that are important to you and investigate opportunities for involvement.

**ACTIVITY 6.7**

## Who Cares About This Issue, and Who Can I Connect With?

Focusing on the issue that you identified in Activity 6.5, find three advocacy organizations that care about your issue (beyond those you already know). A little Internet research will be useful to find the ones most active currently. Complete the following questions for each organization:

| Name and contact of organization | What have they done to advocate for the issue? | What opportunities do they have for me to get involved? (volunteering, letter writing, action alerts, rallies, etc.) |
|---|---|---|
| Org. 1: | | |
| Org. 2: | | |
| Org. 3: | | |

There are many different ways to get involved with advocacy organizations that range in commitment of time, money, and risk. Further, organizations may vary in terms of their approach, some working within the system and some working outside the system. Keeping in mind the principles of solidarity, consider how the organizations you have identified are a part of, or engage with, the communities most affected by the issue you care about. Whether you engage with advocacy organizations as a private citizen or you apply professional or occupational expertise, participating with them can open up new possibilities for social action that you may not have considered, provide avenues for solidarity, and support you in action you take.

## Professional Expertise: White Papers, Amicus Briefs, and Related Strategies

One way to communicate important information with legislators is by providing them with information about an issue from a place of expertise. This is especially relevant if you are in a position where you have expertise or specific training and have access to research and data about a particular issue or outcome. This is helpful to legislators, especially those who support, or may have the potential to support, the position you are advocating. There are several formal documents that are typically used for this purpose including "white papers" and "amicus briefs." White paper is the term used for a document that provides a concise overview of a complex issue using expert knowledge. White papers are intended to help decision and policy makers gain understanding, advocate, or solve a problem. Legislators may welcome and use these documents because they provide concrete data to support arguments that can be used during debates about issues and decisions. Most legislators and their staff don't have time to thoroughly research an issue and don't have expertise in all the areas that come across their desk. White papers can provide this information and help legislators to be more authoritative as well as bring your experience and expertise into the discussion. For example, as a psychologist and counselor, I (Rebecca) work with homeless and near-homeless individuals and families, many of whom are working but the wages are so low that they are unable to pay rent. I have access to research data that outlines this issue, including employment statistics and the impact of underemployment and poverty on wellness and mental health. I can share this with legislators who are considering bills or laws that affect this issue. I can communicate this information either informally through phone calls as described earlier, or I can work with others, such as homelessness advocacy organizations and my professional associations, to develop formal documents to share with legislators.

Another way of contributing expertise is to inform legal proceedings regarding an issue, for example, through an "amicus brief." Amicus briefs are legal documents drafted by parties not directly involved in legal proceedings to provide expertise in a subject being considered in a legal case. Using professional expertise, an amicus brief provides information or arguments to the court for consideration and may also direct the court to consider implications of a legal decision. One example of this was provided by members of the California Psychological Association (CPA) working in collaboration with the American Psychological Association (APA) to shape an amicus brief used in a lawsuit that challenged the constitutionality of a proposition banning same-sex marriage.

> The amicus brief provided extensive psychological research on key points, including how sexual orientation is related to the gender of partners to whom one is attracted—meaning that prohibiting same-sex marriage discriminates on the basis of sexual orientation, rather than just imposing disparate burdens on gay people. (http://www.apa.org/about/offices/ogc/amicus/perry.aspx)

Formal input into legislative and judicial decisions can be an important way to contribute your professional expertise to an issue. It is often best to do that in collaboration with others who can coordinate and add credibility to the message. Many professional organizations have a branch or office that facilitates this kind of advocacy, such as an office of government relations.

## Running for Office

Although this is often the last thing many of us think about, running for political office is possible and can be an important way of contributing to change. Local politics can be a good entry point and can have a significant impact on issues facing your community. The school board, development agency, city council, and other governing bodies may be in a position to make decisions that affect the daily lives of the community. For state-level positions, the Secretary of State website for each state lists all of the political offices and provides valuable voter information. For example, the site for the State of California Secretary of State (http://www.sos.ca.gov/elections/) provides information about each elected position, election and timeline, links for registering to vote, information about lobbying, and much more to help you run for office as well as to be a well-informed participant in the process. There are great resources to help you determine whether running for office is a path you want to pursue, provide both basic and in-depth information to understand the process of running for office, and guidance for getting started. Historically in the United States, elected officials have been overwhelmingly White and male, despite the numerical diversity of their constituencies. There are many reasons for that, including economic capital, historic access to politics and education, attitudes, and policies that have created barriers for participation of women, People of Color, gay and trans individuals, and individuals with disabilities in elected positions. Over the past couple of years, there has been a noticeable increase in organizations working to support individuals from groups that have been underrepresented in politics to help even out the historical imbalance. Below are some examples focused on U.S. elections.

- *Ignite* (http://www.ignitenational.org/our_story)—a nonpartisan, nonprofit organization focusing on encouraging young women to become engaged politically and having unique resources for women in high school and college.

- *Running Start* (https://runningstartonline.org)—a nonpartisan, nonprofit organization supporting young women to get involved in politics.

- *She Should Run* (http://www.sheshouldrun.org/mission)—a nonpartisan, nonprofit organization dedicated to encouraging and supporting women to run for political office.

- *Emily's List* (https://www.emilyslist.org/run-to-win)—political action committee focused on providing training and resources for women in running for political office from a prochoice, Democratic position.

- *The Blue Institute* (https://www.theblue.institute)—to prepare and support more young People of Color into politics in the southern and southwestern United States.

- *CrowdPac* (https://www.crowdpac.com)—a nonpartisan for-profit online resource that allows you to explore the potential of running for office and fundraising.

- *RunForSomething.net*—political action committee focused on assisting young progressives (under age 40) run for office.

Some organizations are partisan. while others are simply focused on increasing representation in government and/or decreasing partisanship. For example, a recent report shared that veterans who are Democrats are entering races for Congress more than ever before. *With Honor*, a cross-partisan organization developed to help veterans interested in running for office, emphasizes that their goal is to "put principles before politics and lead with civility, integrity, and courage, including the courage to meet with someone from another party once a month and sponsor legislation with another party once a year" (https://www.withhonor.org/about-us/our-work).

## ACTIVITY 6.8

### What Would You Run For?

Imagine running for public office. What might your journey be to get there? How might you engage in social action if/when you are elected?

- Would you look at local, state, or national positions?
- What knowledge and skills do you bring to this position?
- What platform would you run on? What issues are most important to you, and what is your position on each of these issues? What informs your position (e.g., data, observation, lived experience)?
- What has your journey been leading up to this path?
- What might your journey be like running for office?

- Can you envision what your campaign speech would look like? What are the keys points you would want to address?
- What would your slogan be? What would your theme song be?

These questions can help you begin to think about making a change through an elected leadership position. This activity also begins to connect the activities you completed earlier in this workbook, such as your values, strengths, building solidarity and relationships, and the elevator speech, and builds on them to work toward specific actions, even if you don't actually run for office.

To influence legislative change, an alternative to running for office is to introduce legislation or initiatives at the state or local level. Some states have a process for citizens to develop and introduce ballot measures or initiatives directly and, through a process, get issues on the ballot for the state voters to decide. In many cases, initiating legislative change may require a critical mass of people, all supporting the need for change. Although this opportunity may not be available in all states, investigating the avenues available in your state can provide some valuable options.

# Working with Groups

The power of numbers cannot be underestimated both in terms of the action and support. As we have discussed in previous sections, the voice of a group will be louder and stronger than your individual voice. Working alongside others in a group can also help build a sense of camaraderie, reduce feelings of isolation, provide role models and opportunities to learn new skills and strategies, pool resources and assets, increase resiliency, and remind you that there are other people who care about the issues you care about. Working effectively with a group is not always easy, but with organization, initiative, flexibility, and a willingness to work on relationships, being a part of a group can be extremely rewarding. Still, some challenges may result due to group and power dynamics, evolving relationships, communication issues, as well as differing goals or strategies among the members. If you are willing to work through these, the benefits are likely to outweigh the challenges.

When working as a part of a group for social action, there are useful considerations. Although on the surface, the group may have come together with a common goal, there are times when individuals or subgroups arise with differing agendas. It can help to identify one goal that can be unifying across everyone in the group, a common goal with a shared definition. This requires not only creating an initial vision and goal setting, but also checking in as the group progresses and engages in social action related to the goal. In addition, you may notice that there are some goals or intentions that are not shared by all. It can be helpful to recognize this and discuss whether this working group is the best place for these other goals. Do these other goals help the group address their shared goal, or does it take the group off track?

In addition to having clarity about a shared goal, setting group rules that everyone can agree on is also important. A collaborative process for developing these rules, or shared understandings, helps to ensure that the rules reflect the culture and needs of the group. For example, "One diva, one mic" is one of many rules identified by Campus Pride (https://www.campuspride.org/resources/ground-rules/) and refers to taking turns speaking. Once established, it is helpful to revisit the rules and consider modifying them as the group evolves. Even with group rules and goals aligned, the reality is that groups are composed of different individuals with different personalities and engagement styles. Remember, this is not a friendship group or your family (although of course there can be overlaps), but rather a goal-driven group. The reality is that you may find some people to be wonderfully engaging and others annoying. Some members may dominate, while others withdraw.

The next several sections explore different types of group action and provide tips for addressing possible challenges that arise. We will also provide resources for more extensive guidance for enhancing the potential of group social action.

## Community Organizing and Coalition Building

Community organizing is a process by which community members come together to address an issue of importance to them. Sometimes it organically arises from the community most affected by an issue (for example, a community that comes together to protest toxic dumping in their community), while other times it is part of a broader campaign that seeks to engage members who may not have been involved or aware of an issue previously (for instance, a national or global environmental protection group). The *Community Toolbox* from the Center for Community Health and Development at the University of Kansas (https://ctb.ku.edu/en) is a great organizing resource that we will mention several times throughout this chapter because it provides practical guidance in so many areas of community organizing.

When individuals organize and work together, they can address power structures that are harder to address when one person works on their own. The Center for Community Change states that,

> Community organizing almost always includes confrontation of some sort. The people who want something get themselves together to ask for it, often the people who could give them what they want get jumpy. Community organizing strategies include meeting with corporate or government decision makers to hold them accountable for their actions, designing programs for others (not the group) to implement that meet the needs of the community, and aggressive group action to block negative developments or behaviors (highway construction that leads to neighborhood destruction, etc.). (http://comm-org.wisc.edu/ papers97/beckwith.htm)

Community organizing involves the skills one uses in bringing people together (e.g., motivating, public speaking, networking) as a community member or even one's paid job. In 2009, the *New York Times* declared community organizing as an "enviable" career and described its growing popularity, especially given President Obama's history as a community organizer (https://www.nytimes.com/2009/04/12/fashion/12organizer.html). The article highlighted a number of people who had chosen organizing as a career path given their values, their religious or spiritual commitment, or inspiration from role models and leaders.

Understanding community organizing, and the related skills and strategies, is important even if most of us are not engaging in community organizing as a career or occupation. The process and strategies of organizing vary somewhat, depending on several conditions: Is it a pre-established issue and group? Are they organizing to rally greater numbers of people and raise awareness? Or is this a groundswell of people who see an issue and are working together to create solutions? In a pre-established group, there is often a preexisting structure, and the task may be to help convey an issue, potential solutions, and meaning in order to motivate others to participate. In the case where community comes together as an emerging part of an empowered change process, it may be necessary for the group to define a workable structure, guidelines, vision, and goals for the group, in addition to the action they plan and carry out to address their issue. In other words, being an effective group requires work beyond the group's social action. Regardless of the form, developing relationships, identifying common goals, negotiating, evaluating success, creative problem solving, and action planning are useful.

Coalition building is one strategy of community organizing. Coalitions are groups that are formed when people or groups of people come together around a central issue and shared goal. The coalition may be created as a temporary group or an ongoing group that expects to evolve over time as it continues to work on the issue. Coalitions may be formal or informal, and may be very specific in terms of expertise and membership, or they may be very diverse. One advantage of creating or joining a diverse coalition is that members bring different skill sets and different connections that can be essential to the effort. A coalition can be made up of individuals representing different perspectives or made up of groups who have shared investment or interest. For example, imagine that your community has seen an increase in racist graffiti. You might reach out to community members, including the school board, local businesses, and local politicians, as well as national groups such as the Southern Poverty Law Center and the NAACP. Perhaps a group in the school board is committed to working on making the school a more positive place for all students; the local businesses want the community to project an image of a welcoming place; and local politicians would like to be responsive to their constituents who are feeling less safe in their district. In your conversations, you might identify a shared commitment to publicly addressing such acts of hate vandalism and making your community a more welcoming place. Together, your group is able to bring together different skills, resources, and connections in the community as well as widen the circle through your respective connections.

There are a number of tips that can be useful for more effective coalition building:

1. establish common values and interests as well as areas where there might be differences;
2. determine how the group will function together (e.g., will there be representatives, will the group meet regularly, will there be a leader or will that be a shared role, who will take on various roles?);
3. talk about who needs to be represented (who is most affected by the issue and thus has insight), who has power, who is not present and why, and how to make the group accessible?;
4. establish short- and long-term goals;
5. create a plan of action with commitment from members; and
6. implement, then assess, how the goals were met.

*The Community Toolbox* provides more guidance for when and how to establish a coalition, who is important to have represented, barriers or potential problems that might arise, and other essential information.

Thinking about working together with others can feel inspiring for some and daunting for others. Being thoughtful about bringing together an effective group is a good start. In the next activity, practice thinking through coalition building as a strategy for social action.

### ACTIVITY 6.9

### Simulation 1: Who's on the Team?

Choose one of the issues you identified as a priority in Activity 6.5. Consider how a coalition might be helpful in addressing some aspect of that issue. If there is already a group working on that issue, think about how to expand or start a local coalition to take action.

- What is the issue?
- Who ought to be a part of your coalition?
  - Who cares about the issue?
  - Who has needed skills to collaboratively plan and carry out action?
  - Who has intimate knowledge and lived experience related to the issue?
  - Who has power (in the community, at decision making levels, etc.)?
- How might you reach out to these potential team members?
- How could an elevator speech be helpful?

## Organizing Community Events

Perhaps one of the strategies that might be most familiar to you if you have ever participated with your school, religious or spiritual organization, or other community group is that of creating and holding events, whether as fundraisers, celebrations, or community gatherings. Talents in organizing events (sometimes called event planning) can be enormously useful for bringing people together around an issue, sharing concerns, raising awareness, and amplifying a message to be heard beyond the group. Some examples of social action–oriented community events include "town hall" meetings, education events, community dialogues, campaigns, art-making events, actions (e.g., protests, teach-ins, etc.), ceremonies, and fundraisers. For example, a friend of ours and his partner hold "Speakeasy Karaoke" events that they do in their home or other venues. They invite community members and progressive politicians for community building, fundraising, and to raise awareness about issues that are important to diverse groups and to engage support for the politicians' campaigns. This allows them to do important work, but also to enjoy the time together singing karaoke. There are a lot of great resources providing guidance for planning events, including those focused on social action such as the Youth Activist Toolkit (http://www.advocatesforyouth.org/publications/publications-a-z/2229-youth-activists-toolkit), Beautiful Rising (https://beautifultrouble.org), and the Community Toolbox (https://ctb.ku.edu/en). We will highlight some basics here and later ask you to think about how you might apply these in creating an event for one of the issues you have identified.

When planning a community event, the process of determining who should be involved as leaders, planners, and decision makers is critical. This may be easier if you are a part of the community. If you are not, the principle of solidarity resurfaces again as communities who care about the issue should be important contributors as planners and participants. Keep in mind that the people who are willing and interested in planning may be motivated by different things than the participants you hope to attract.

In the next activity, you will create a single event for social action and strategies for getting the word out about the event. The following questions can be helpful in approaching the process of planning an event and vary depending on the type of event and goals.

## ACTIVITY 6.10

### Planning a Community Event

For this activity, name an issue you have identified as a priority. Answer the questions below and sketch out ideas for this event. Consider what you already know and what you don't know. Also, consider who may be able to assist and/or lead this effort.

1. *Goals:* What is your group trying to accomplish? What are the goals for the event? (For example, raising funds? Raising awareness? Making a statement? Bringing people together? Celebrating?)
2. *Resources:* Who is the community? What skills and knowledge should be represented on the organizing team (e.g., a group facilitator, someone to keep the timeline and tasks on track, someone to keep different aspects of the community engaged and informed, someone to communicate with the media, someone to enlist volunteers, security, and so on)? What is the budget, and are there sources for additional resources (e.g., donations of art supplies, food, lumber, etc.)?
3. *Timeline:* What is the best timing given the purpose, goals, and tasks that need to be completed?
4. *Logistics:* What are the facility needs (size of place, restrooms, etc.)? How many people do you need for the day of the event? Do you need permits or involvement of city or neighborhood

authorities? How will you minimize the risk of injury? How will you maximize accessibility?

5. **Outcomes:** What are the possible outcomes (positive and negative) on the day of the event and following the event?

6. **Attendees:** Whom do you want to attend, and how many? Whom do you want to hear about this, and what message do you want them to hear? What media would bring the most and best attention to your event and your issue (think about the demographics of the participants you hope to attend and what media is most likely to be used)? What would motivate them to attend?

7. **Publicizing the event:** Create an announcement (either a press release, a flyer, or social media announcement) to get your message across and motivate people to attend. How would you disseminate it? Who can help with this?

8. **Follow-up:** What kind of follow-up can you do with the community, media, decision makers, etc., to continue progress on the goals?

Many times, we are interested in engaging in these events but are not prepared to be the leader. It is most helpful to think of the group as a team where everyone is a member and can take on various roles in their pursuit of a shared goal. Open discussion about roles, expectations, leadership, and communication styles can be very helpful. Sometimes assigning a facilitator role or bringing in an outside facilitator can help create a supportive, effective, and well-functioning team. Guidelines for effective group functioning discussed throughout this section on Working with Groups can be useful for all kinds of groups.

## Not Everyone Needs to Be a Leader

One of the myths about social action is that in order to make a difference, you need to be the one making things happen. Although there is a need for leadership, there is also a need for followership. Uhl-Bien, Riggio, Lowe, and Carsten (2014) describe the role of followers in any organization and suggest that the follower role is more important than has been given credit before. They describe three ways that shape the behavior of followers, including passive, anti-authoritarian, and proactive. Passive followers work to implement the initiatives and directives of the leaders. Anti-authoritarian followers (or "non-followers") resist any direction and may work against the leadership. The proactive approach is seen as followers take initiative, question, and participate with leadership. They suggest that the passive and proactive follower approaches are necessary, and the appropriate role depends on the person and the circumstances. We are going to suggest that there is perhaps a more important reason for taking a follower role, particularly if you are not a member of the community most affected by the issue you are working on or if you are new to an organization. You may have grown up with cultural values that emphasize a respect for observation, silence, learning from elders, and reserving critique. Or you may have grown up with cultural values that emphasize vocal dissent, challenge, competition, and independence. When you look back to the section on "Strength and Positionality" in Chapter 4, you may recall the discussion about the role our experiences and our identities play and the importance of attending to our position, power, and privilege in relation to the group or issue we may be concerned about. Also, as discussed in Chapter 5 on Solidarity, we need to consider the roles of cultural humility, allies and accomplices, and liberation and how those relate to leadership as well as how to support others in leadership roles.

## A Note About Roles and Group Dynamics

Working with others is critical for the success of social action. Group dynamics exist whenever people come together, whether the purpose is to achieve a goal or simply to spend time together. These dynamics include how individuals talk to each other, the spoken and unspoken rules and patterns of behavior, and the roles that each member takes (intentionally or unintentionally). Understanding and managing groups can increase the likelihood of success in whatever strategy you undertake. The influence of organizational politics in navigating and planning social action cannot be overstated. In his article in the *Harvard Review*, Michael Jarrett, a professor of organizational behavior, talks about four different types of organizational politics and uses the metaphors of weeds, rocks, high ground, and woods to describe the dynamics and recommend strategies for dealing with each type (https://hbr.org/2017/04/the-4-types-of-organizational-politics). The "weeds" are informal networks of individuals that grow naturally in an organization and can address problems as they come up, but unchecked may become matted and tangled. "Rocks" are individuals who are formalized in their position within the organization, such as a manager, a chair of a committee or task force, the communications person, or others. The rocks can provide stability and visible support for an idea or action, or they can block action. The "high ground" represents formal and visible structures or rules at an organizational level; for example, the vision statement. This can be helpful in providing consistency, clarity, and stability but can also result in bureaucracy. "Woods" are informal organizational level guidelines, sometimes unwritten rules, that can be helpful but can also create blocks if you don't know them. Understanding how to work with each of these structures can make the difference between productively working with others and getting stuck.

# Communicating With and Through Media

Media can be used to inform, persuade, and motivate people through news-papers, television, podcasts, social media, and social media influencers, among others. The skill and commitment needed for using media for social action ranges widely from very little to sophisticated. For more strategic and longer-term change, more intentionality and expertise are needed regarding how to engage with media, the types of media used, and how media fits into a larger effort. In this section, we will touch on the basics for engaging with existing media sources, and in a later section, we talk about opportunities to create media yourself.

## Media Interviews

Whether as a citizen or an expert, being interviewed by television, print media, or Internet venues such as podcasts or web series provide opportunities to share your perspective and knowledge. The way you approach these varies depending on the circumstances: for example, planned or unplanned, as a member of the public or as an expert, a brief response or a full interview, adversarial or collaborative. If you are preparing to be interviewed as a professional or a person with expertise, a professional association may be a good resource for guidance. For example, the American Psychological Association provides a resource, "How to Work with the Media" that outlines different circumstances such as television, radio, and print interviews where we speak on behalf of an organization or issue (http://www.apa.org/pubs/authors/media/index.aspx).

When preparing for a media interview, one of the considerations is to determine which interviews are appropriate and a good fit for your message and intent. What is the source (in other words, what paper, web-site, podcast, news show, etc.)? What is the context (e.g., are you being brought in as an expert, a representative of an issue or organization)? What are the stories and the perspectives typically taken by this source and this interviewer? What is the story they are hoping to get? Who else are they interviewing for this story? Who is the audience? Will you have an opportunity to review or amend your comments after the interview is completed? Is this an individual interview, or will they have a panel? If it is a panel, who else will be on the panel? Do your research and remember that sometimes an interview is simply for information; other times it is to present opposing views. It is your right to request information prior to the interview and hope the information they give you is accurate so you can make an informed decision about whether and how to participate.

After considering these questions, you can decide if this is an appropriate opportunity. If so, it is time to prepare. Some interviews will involve a "pre-interview," where the interviewer explores some of the questions with you prior to the actual interview. In some cases, it may be appropriate for you to request sample questions or the actual list of questions prior to the interview. In a print interview or prerecorded interview, you may have the opportunity to review what will be used.

There are some basic tips for preparing for the interview, including writing out talking points, ensuring you have some basic supporting evidence for your points, preparing a very short illustration or story, and brainstorming possible unexpected questions. The principle of staying focused on the issue that you wish to address is critical. Decide where your boundaries of expertise lie and how you will handle things if the interview veers into areas that you do not have expertise or have not really prepared. When we say expertise, we mean your knowledge gained through experience and training as well as the position you represent if speaking on behalf of an organization or issue. Being caught by surprise and trying to answer without being clear of your position can sometimes end with undesirable results. It may be helpful to even practice your talking points and illustrations, ensuring they are brief, clear, and to the point. Consider enlisting the help of a friend or two as an audience to provide honest feedback to you. If you are speaking on behalf of a group, practicing with someone from that group may be helpful to increase the chances you are representing their position.

So far, we have mostly talked about interviews that are planned. In other cases, the interview may be unexpected, with little or no time to prepare; for example, if you are approached on the street as a member of the public or as an event attendee and asked your opinion or reaction to something. You can choose "no comment" or to respond. A few years ago, my (Rebecca's) family and I were in Columbus Circle in Manhattan and CNN stopped us to ask about our opinion about airport scanners and privacy. They interviewed my partner, and we later talked about the challenge of articulating thoughts in a way that wouldn't convey alarmist attitudes or buy into any political perspective unknowingly. My partner had said on camera that he knew that some people were concerned about privacy, but that he didn't think the scanners were a privacy problem. When the interview was televised, the portion that was selected was just the quote of "some people are concerned about privacy" and neglected his actual opinion. It was frustrating but a relatively minor issue. We noticed that the quotes that were selected for that news piece seemed to build a particular story overall and wondered if they selected quotes to draw the story they intended from the beginning rather than a random poll. One thing is for certain: television and radio commentary always has a time constraint, and thus it is likely that any footage will be cut into smaller pieces. Keeping your message very short and direct can help. Providing context, although very helpful in a conversation, may end up getting cut when your interview is aired.

As an expert or known scholar in a particular area, you may also be contacted unexpectedly by the media. This often happens in response to an event and the news source is seeking "expert" opinions or reactions to the event to help inform, present different sides of an issue, or liven up a story. Sometimes, it is not completely unexpected, but there is very little notice nonetheless. In these situations, making decisions about what areas of expertise you have and what you feel comfortable sharing is helpful prior to being interviewed. As an expert in a subject, you are likely to be more informed than the general public about an issue or event but not necessarily have your thoughts articulated in a "media-ready" response. Although it is difficult to always be ready, there are some basic things you can do. First, know the scope of your expertise, and stick to that. There are a number of ways that you can be identified as an "expert" on a topic, most commonly through your employer or professional association (make sure you understand their policies regarding public appearances first). For example, as faculty at universities, we are sometimes approached by media to comment on a particular issue or story using our "expert" knowledge. The public relations office of the university keeps a database of faculty and researchers who are willing to talk with media on specific topics. Second, if you are approached for a response (and it is within your expertise), if you do not do this on a regular basis, it is fine to tell the inquirer that you would be happy to talk to them at a specific scheduled time. Further, ask them to provide some background information on their source and story. It may risky to do the interview on the spot unless you understand the context, source, and feel very comfortable with what you will say. At the same time, they might need the story right away and thus you might miss the opportunity to speak out. Often, the interviewer has a very short window in which to get an interview, so be aware that you may need to be flexible. Third, when there is an event that likely may generate media attention, you may prepare some very brief talking points, or even contact media proactively. These types of talking points can also be used when writing op-eds and letters to the editor. Contacting media proactively can be an important form of advocacy by sharing a perspective or bringing an otherwise ignored story or issue to the surface.

Panel interviews present unique challenges and opportunities. Depending on the media outlet, a panel may be intended to present different expertise on the same topic, or to set up a debate with opposing viewpoints. There are many considerations when deciding whether to participate in this type of format, and it is likely that the discussion will move beyond prepared questions and responses. The following information can help you decide whether you are willing to participate. Who are the other presenters, and what might their positions be? In viewing past situations involving this moderator or news source, how does the moderator typically engage, and do they have a particular angle? What expertise or position are you expected to bring, is it within your scope, and how does that fit with the program or moderator's perspective? How comfortable are you at politely interrupting people or talking over people if there is a dominating panel member or moderator? How comfortable are you with confrontational discussions? Whether the interview is a surprise, or you initiate the interview, being prepared can make a difference in how well you use the opportunity for social action. The next activity is designed to give you some practice in preparing for a media interview.

### ACTIVITY 6.11

## One Media Source and Three Talking Points

For this activity, imagine that you would like to be interviewed about an issue you care about.

1. Choose one of your high-priority issues and think about the information you have about that topic, including research, statistics, and stories.
2. Identify one news source that might be interested in a story about your issue (television, radio, newspaper, etc.). Consider the audience: what would capture their attention? Is the audience likely to agree with you or be opposed to your opinion?
3. Now, develop a statement to summarize the issue and three talking points conveying why this is an issue and what should happen. It helps to use at least one set of compelling statistics and one story to illustrate how the issue affects people.

Issue:
Talking point 1 (statistics):
Talking point 2 (story):
Talking point 3 (what you want to see happen):

***Example: Rebecca and racist graffiti***

Issue: Racism in our community, specifically symbols of hate including graffiti
Talking point 1: There were four examples of racist graffiti last year in the

high school and middle school that were reported by the local newspaper. According to the Southern Poverty Law Center, two out of three hate crimes go unreported, and schools have been the most common place where hate crimes have been seen. Therefore, it is likely that many more incidences occur in our local schools than are reported. Studies reported by the American Psychological Association have shown that students who face acts of discrimination experience higher stress levels and more health problems.

Talking point 2: I have two White teenage children who go to school at the high school, and when I asked them about the graffiti, they said, "That stuff happens all the time—it hardly ever gets reported, and teachers often miss it or don't say anything."

Talking point 3: The community and the school need to take these seriously and consider the impact on all students and community members. A strong initiative of action and training is needed for school staff to recognize racism and know how to respond.

Even a little preparation can help gather your thoughts and allow you to create a clearer and more intentional message. There are other ways of engaging with media that allow you more space and time to refine your message and ensure that more voices are heard.

## Op-Eds: Opinion Editorials

Op-eds are an opportunity to write from a place of expertise in the hopes of reaching a general audience through a news source. It is similar to a news column in that it contains facts and substantive information, yet it is different in that it clearly comes from a particular point of view. We may question whether news columns actually contain facts and provide an unbiased perspective on news, especially given the trend and proliferation of "news" that is based more on opinion but presented as fact. Nonetheless, let's assume "news" and op-eds share the use of facts and data. Letters to the editor and op-eds are similar in that they both seek to communicate a perspective or opinion. They differ in that the writing of the op-ed should have professional expertise and facts regarding the topic, whereas the letter to the editor need not come from an expert but instead could be an interested member of the public.

There are a number of good resources for writing op-eds, and they share similar strategies (https://www.nytimes.com/2017/08/25/opinion/tips-for-aspiring-op-ed-writers.html; https://shorensteincenter.org/wp-content/up-loads/2012/07/HO_NEW_HOW-TO-WRITE-AN-OPED-OR-COLUMN.pdf; https://apps.carleton.edu/media_relations/about/op_ed_guidelines/; http://www.apa.org/monitor/2018/02/write-op-ed.aspx). First, be clear about your purpose in writing this piece. What do you want the reader to come away with? Be clear about the audience you are trying to reach and what venue or source is the best way to reach this audience. Second, become familiar with the publication you want to target; what types of articles and op-eds do they publish? What are their instructions for op-ed authors (length of article, process for submission, other suggestions or requirements)? As you write the actual piece, consider some common recommendations. Begin the article with a "hook"—in other words, you want the reader to know your purpose and to care about it enough to keep reading. End your piece with a call to action. The guide from the Harvard Kennedy School describes the usefulness of beginning with a "strong claim, a surprising fact, a metaphor, a mystery, or a counter-intuitive observation that entices the reader into reading more" (https://shorensteincenter.org/wp-content/uploads/2012/07/HO_NEW_HOW-TO-WRITE-AN-OPED-OR-COLUMN.pdf). Next, make your point, and then use the op-ed to substantiate each aspect of your point using data and research. The American Psychological Association's guide for op-eds suggests leading with your conclusion, in contrast to the usual way journal articles or research typically build toward the conclusion (http://www.apa.org/monitor/2018/02/write-op-ed.aspx). In an op-ed, use data, quotes, and facts that are likely to be perceived as credible, without being excessive. Limit the amount of information you provide to what is necessary to make a strong point. Use language and a writing style that is familiar to the audience and avoid jargon and clichés. Weaving a narrative or story into the substantive information can help the facts and data come alive. Each major point should be stated, then substantiated and supported. A strong ending for the op-ed is critical and should reiterate the main objective, preferably in a way the reader can understand more deeply given the material you have provided in the article. Be clear about what should happen or what action the reader can take. Once the article is written, make sure to proofread (even get friends and colleagues to read and provide feedback). You are looking for clarity, persuasiveness, and strength. Finally, make sure to only submit to one source at a time. If you don't hear back from them within a reasonable amount of time (often indicated in their guidelines), then follow up with them and ask when a decision will be made. Inform them that if it is not accepted, you would like to submit it to another source.

## Letters to the Editor

Letters to the editor have a long history in newspapers and magazines as a way for readers and the general public to respond to current issues in their local community or nation. A letter to the editor can inform, present arguments, start a community conversation, keep an issue alive, or respond to a published story or to a previously published letter to the editor. It is a way of having a conversation in a big venue with the benefit of allowing you to have the time to thoughtfully put your words together in a way that conveys your message. There are some great resources to use when developing a letter to the editor, and we suggest that you refer to those for more thorough guidance (for example, https://ctb.ku.edu/en/table-of-contents/ advocacy/direct-action/letters-to-editor/main). Most importantly, you will want the letter to convey a concise and clear message. We will share some basics here to get you started. The following is an outline suggested by one of our favorite resources—the Community Toolbox (https://ctb.ku.edu/en).

- Begin with a salutation such as "Dear Editor" (like in a letter).

- Hook the reader by starting with a powerful sentence or two to let the reader know why you are writing and to capture their interest.

- Briefly (one or two sentences) describe why this issue is important to the reader. Think about your audience; why is this relevant for them? Explain the issue in a way that will make sense to them.

- If you are writing about something that has already happened, such as a decision or event, describe the outcome and its impact on the reader. If at all possible, use evidence.

- Concisely state what you think should happen. If you are writing to praise or acknowledge something positive, you can suggest steps to take this further. If you are criticizing something that has happened, describe what you think needs to be done to fix it. Be as specific as possible with actionable steps that the reader can take.

Letters to the editor should be short, clear, and appropriate for their audience. It is also helpful to keep the language constructive in nature. The source you are aiming for most likely has specific guidelines (e.g., number of words or characters) for letters and the process for submission and review. In the next activity, you will write a letter to the editor of a news source about one of your issues of concern.

### ACTIVITY 6.12

### One Letter

For this activity, you will draft a letter to a news source (e.g., newspaper, magazine, etc.) about a real issue you care about.

1. Choose an appropriate news source and find out their guidelines for letters to the editor (guidelines are usually published on their website).

2. Use the following outline to create a structure for the information and points you will include in your letter.
3. Transform your outline into a narrative letter form.
4. Have someone read the letter and give you feedback. Is your point clear? Is it readable? Do they finish the article knowing what you think should happen? Do they feel inclined to take action?

**Consider the sample outline below:**

Dear Editor,

- A powerful sentence or two to let the reader know why you are writing and capture their interest; this is your hook.
- Describe why this issue is important to the reader.
- What is the issue? Is your letter about something that happened recently? What was the result?
- What do you think should happen? What should the reader do next?

Letters to the editor can express your personal voice or professional voice. Sometimes, we just need to get the word out about an action or an issue. Letters to the editor can be a forum for this, but there are also approaches such as press releases that are a bit briefer and can encourage a news source to pick up a story about an action or an event.

# Press Releases

A press release is a very brief announcement about an event that is scheduled to take place (or has taken place), new developments in an issue or information, or other newsworthy items. This is an opportunity to alert your community (or a broader audience) to an issue and action being taken about that issue. The advantage of a press release is that it allows the community to present an issue, event, or situation in the way that they think is most accurate and useful. Press releases are typically one or two pages long and are targeted toward newspaper or magazine editors (traditional or online) and broadcast radio producers with the goal of generating interest in a story, event, or issue resulting in a follow-up story or reporting on your event.

There are a number of great resources online for writing a press release, and most include the following basic guidelines. Begin with a clear and compelling headline and dateline (the date and city where the press release originates). In the body, begin with a strong opening sentence followed by a few sentences presenting the story and why it matters. Be sure to include a summary of organizations involved and your contact information so reporters and news sources can follow up.

## Holding Media Accountable

At the local level, there is the potential for engaging and collaborating with media to influence local, state, and national issues. Media, including television, radio, email, and social media, has the potential to inform or misinform the public. One important avenue for action is holding media accountable. For example, in April 2018, *Deadspin* exposed a coordinated effort of Sinclair media to require news anchors at its local stations to recite an identical speech warning about fake news and news agencies reporting without fact checking, echoing accusations of the U.S. president. The company owned 190 stations and was in the process of acquiring dozens more (https://www.npr.org/sections/thetwo-way/2018/04/02/598794433/video-reveals-power-of-sinclair-as-local-news-anchors-recite-script-in-unison). This proliferation of a specific message to local communities illustrates coordinated efforts to influence public perception that likely extends to a number of issues through a perceived credible news source. One of the challenges of the rapid recirculation of messages in media is that the more often the message is repeated, the more it is presented as fact. We can hold media accountable in a variety of ways, ranging from writing a letter to the editor, alerting the public to the misinformation, boycotting the source, contacting the station or publisher, contacting advertisers, and many others. Many of these strategies are more powerful when acting as a group but can also be done individually.

Communicating with media is one way of communicating with the public. In the next section, we describe other strategies worth considering as well.

# Communicating With the Public

A powerful force in social change is the momentum and support of the public. At the same time, injustice is perpetuated and maintained by members of the public. Actions that inform and influence public opinion can help to make lasting change. Many of the strategies that are most visible are those that influence the public; for example, demonstrations, rallies, public art, and the use of media.

## Public Displays of Resistance

Rallies, marches, hunger strikes, sit-ins, and teach-ins are probably the most familiar forms of resistance, given that they tend to generate large-scale publicity and media attention. In the United States, there has been a re-surgence of public demonstrations with greater visibility, including Black Lives Matter, the Women's March, March for our Lives, the Prison Strike, People's Climate March, March for Science, and many others. There are also quieter and equally powerful public displays of resistance, such as those in visual art, murals, performance art, and craftivism.

The Virtual Knowledge Centre to End the Violence toward Women and Girls, an online guide from the United Nations-Women (http://www.end-vawnow.org/en/articles/1297-demonstrations-marches-and-rallies.html), suggests that there are three types of situations in which demonstrations may be a useful approach:

1. when there is a large number of people who are likely to participate;
2. when the demonstration is linked to a wider campaign; and
3. when there is an imminent decision or vote that may be influenced by the kind of message a demonstration can bring.

The Virtual Knowledge Centre guide provides important considerations regarding demonstrations and a checklist for organizing a rally, march, or demonstration, including planning, collaboration, and a multitude of steps to increase the likelihood that the message is conveyed as intended and heard by the intended audience. Further, careful planning can minimize harm that may come to marchers and the public and link to more extended action. If a public demonstration seems to be the best strategy for an issue you have identified, it helps to work with others and begin planning far in advance. If you are new to organizing, we suggest you use one of the many tools and tips available from activists who have been engaged in organizing successful events.

In addition to impacting state and national policy decisions, citizen activism can also influence local, state, and national elections, according to a 2018 Stanford University study by Daniel Gilliom and Sarah Soule. Public demonstrations such as large-scale strategies, rallies, and marches also provide great opportunities for everyday social action.

### EXAMPLE

## Rebecca

Participating in public demonstrations or rallies is useful for my own sustain-ability and helps me to feel energized and connected to people who share my concerns and values, at least in some way. The neighborhood I live in is not an activist community and being around people who do not share the same passions for social action can feel isolating. Public demonstrations provide a great avenue to feel solidarity, channel anger and frustration, feel the power of a group, and remind me that there are people who care about this issue and are doing something about it. Participating in rallies and large demonstrations also connects me with information, issues, leaders, and inspirational change agents that I may not have been familiar with and provides avenues for follow-up and more sustained action. For example, if I attend a climate march, it is likely that there will be people from a variety of different climate organizations present who are able to provide me with the opportunity to find new connections, new resources, new information about issues I care about, and opportunities for future engagement.

Marches, rallies, and demonstrations can be exciting, exhilarating, and meaningful forms of resistance. To be most effective, there are some things that are helpful to remember, specifically in terms of access, messaging, and safety. Access and participation in marches or rallies can be challenging for people who have difficulty getting around, anxiety or fear in crowds, or other issues. In addition, for people who live in small communities, there may be few opportunities close by. Thus, participating in a big demonstration may require traveling, more logistics, and careful planning.

Demonstrations and rallies are powerful, and organizers typically try to help keep the focus of the message through speakers, signs, pre-event material, and other communications. Yet, in a large group, we don't have full control of the message that is conveyed by the demonstration or by individuals involved. Because a large demonstration typically involves a diverse group of people with varying opinions and approaches, there is a chance that some people participating may have different ideas about what the message should be, how those in power should be challenged, and how to engage with police or others who might oppose the demonstrators.

Whenever one chooses to participate in a crowd, there are safety reminders that are helpful to consider. This is particularly the case when there is a possibility of people who oppose the group's message. The large majority of demonstrations are peaceful with little concern for safety, although taking some of the same precautions you might use while traveling to a new place is a good rule of thumb (for example, don't carry valuables, do carry water, have a phone, let someone know where you are). On rare occasions, it may be helpful to be prepared for the unexpected. Several websites provide helpful hints, such as Amnesty International's guide for preparing to participate in demonstrations (https://www.amnestyusa.org/pdfs/SafeyDuringProtest_F. pdf). Another article, from the American Civil Liberties Union (ACLU), summarizes tips regarding your free speech rights and how those might be relevant when participating in demonstrations (https://qz.com/890689/what-us-protestors-can-and-cannot-do-according-to-the-aclu/).

One final note about participating in demonstrations is that some people, due to their cultural identity and discrimination based on the way they look, may be more at risk than others. Similarly, depending on the focus of the demonstration (for example, demonstrations focusing on racialized violence) and context (a community that disagrees with the focus of the demonstration, for instance), there may be a higher likelihood of police action or opposition to the protest and thus a greater likelihood of hostility. Unfortunately, people who tend to be targets of violence and oppression (e.g., undocumented individuals, transgender individuals, People of Color, Indigenous people), whether by police or the general public, may want to consider having a stronger safety plan, more allies in the demonstration, or consider other ways of taking action if a demonstration presents too many risks or is inaccessible. There are opportunities to participate in demonstrations safely whether in the midst of a crowd or supporting from behind the scenes.

In addition to direct action, a well-organized public display of resistance includes forethought about how to help participants heal and rejuvenate after taking action. The *Healing Action Toolkit* from Black Lives Matter (https://blacklivesmatter.com/resource/healing-action-toolkit/) suggests that a part of organizing can include reaching out to healers in the community who may be willing to provide support during or after actions. Finding one or more healers who are willing to coordinate other folks from their network can be extremely helpful, especially when the public action is large scale and requiring intense emotional and/or physical engagement. Some examples include having counselors onsite or on call, food drop-offs, legal support, medical support, acupuncture, massage, foot care, and others.

## Art

Visual and performance art and craftivism can be unique forms of public displays of activism and resistance. Art has been used for centuries to tell stories and communicate messages visually and emotionally. In the present day, visual resistance art can be seen in posters, banners, murals, and monuments, as well as online through social media and web venues. Art can send a message, bring feelings to the surface, and make the invisible, visible in ways that words cannot. The process of making resistance art can also function to bring people together, build solidarity, and enhance community voices. In a recent article about monuments that honor gender and sexual minority individuals, psychologists Joseph Orangias, Jeannie Simms, and Sloane French (2017) point out that monuments can provide visibility and reduce stigma, educate the public about historical oppression, and prompt public debate and discussion regarding current struggles.

One of the most powerful uses of art as activism is when it provides a platform for people who are most impacted by an issue to raise awareness and have a voice. Like many other urban communities, the San Francisco Bay Area is home to incredible murals that portray resilience and resistance. Lori Flores, an associate professor of history at Stony Brook University, describes the significance of the murals of the Mission District, a historically Latino community in San Francisco, their place in activism, and the threat presented by gentrification in that neighborhood (https://boomcalifornia.com/2017/03/06/seeing-through-murals-the-future-of-latino-san-francisco/). Another powerful mural, *Maestrapeace*, adorns the Women's Building in San Francisco. This mural was created by Latina and Indigenous women muralists in the 1990s and depicts activists and ancestors inspiring and communicating the impact and ongoing influence of leaders and community members as well as "envisions a world healed of injustices" (Alicia et al., 2019). Oakland, across the bay from San Francisco and home to Black Lives Matter, hosts some amazing murals recounting the activism of predominantly African American communities. The Oakland Super Heroes Mural Project (http://www.ahc-oakland.org/oakland-mural-project-1) is "a crucial community development effort by Attitudinal Healing Connection (AHC) in Oakland that will engage over 300 youth to be change-agents in their community. This project aims to resolve issues that plague our city, create over 30 jobs, enhance our neighborhoods and reduce blight." *Participatory media* is a term that has been used for this approach. Similar to murals, photovoice projects also provide a venue for individuals and communities to document their reality and share it. One such example is found in "Shooting Back" (https://shootingback.net), a project founded by Jim Hubbard, a photojournalist, that partners with Indigenous communities and homeless communities to bring cameras and photography to youth who then document their world.

Craftivism is another form of using art, specifically handcrafting, in activism as a way to convey messages. Sarah Corbett, in her TED Talk about the need for introverts in activism, describes a range of crafted messages as a "gentler form of activism" (https://www.ted.com/talks/sarah_corbett_activism_needs_introverts). Some of the campaigns she describes include handwritten notes placed into clothing describing the working conditions of garment workers and embroidered handkerchiefs with messages given to executives of a clothing retailer to advocate for a living wage for employees. Sarah emphasizes that this approach was meant to raise awareness and start conversations in a collaborative way, with the assumption that the receiver of these messages would "want" to do the "right thing" and needed encouragement to do so.

Art as activism can also be heard through spoken word, poetry, song, storytelling, theater, and performance art. *Theater of the Oppressed* is an approach developed by Augusto Boal in Brazil in the 1970s as a method for people to engage with the theater process in a way that facilitates them in critically analyzing the structures and systems that impact their lives, then envision a desired future. Based on the work of a number of other scholars, educators, and community organizers, most notably Paolo Freire, this approach is meant to subvert and make visible the systems that shape and constrain communities that are harmed by forces such as poverty, oppression, discrimination, unemployment, and other results of inequity. Further, the process of engaging in the theater is meant to draw spectators into action, to help them to see how they are also affected by these forces, and to become active in addressing issues that are important to them.

A number of artists share their perspectives on the use of spoken art as resistance. Marcus Ellsworth, a spoken word artist, describes the power of art in activism to bring people together and raise awareness (https://www. youtube.com/watch?reload=9&v=KLg8LMK_Ct4). Further, Kyle "Guante" Tran Myhre (https://www.youtube.com/watch?v=6Zex8K6h_jk), a poetry slam champion, activist, and educator, talks about the use of poetry and art to open conversations striving for greater understanding rather than having answers. Marquese McFerguson, in his TED Talk on art, social change, and uncomfortable conversations, describes the power of storytelling to help people shift their perspective and better understand experiences of people who are different from them. He emphasizes the power of storytelling in building bridges and leading to being better allies (https://www.youtube. com/watch?v=xjQRWWdocwg).

Fortunately, the examples of art to increase understanding and aware-ness are too numerous to discuss here. There are thousands of examples of art as activism globally that have impacted social change. Some of these can be seen in the Design Museum's 2018 exhibit, "Hope to Nope: Graphics and Politics 2008–2018," which chronicles resistance art glob-ally (https://designmuseum.org/exhibitions/hope-to-nope-graphics-and-politics-2008-18). For this next activity, you will look beyond the sources listed above and find inspiration through activist art to help communicate about issues you care about.

**ACTIVITY 6.13**

**Discovering the Art of Activism**

**Option 1:** Find three pieces of art (visual, spoken, or performance) that relate to one of the issues you prioritized. Examine each piece with the following questions:

- how does it evoke emotion?
- what is the message?
- what is the desired outcome of the piece?
- how might it move someone to take action?
- how could the piece be more effective for social change?

**Option 2:** Create a poster regarding your issue or for an event to inform or activate. Consider how the visuals you present can tap into the viewer's (or listener's) emotion to trigger action or thought. The questions above can help you consider how your art piece can convey your message and move the viewer.

# Blogs, Podcasts, and Other Digital Media

The vibrancy of digital communication has opened up a world of possibilities for sharing issues, perspectives, information, and for building community. Social media in general has the potential to connect people, inspire, and share information as well as proliferate hostility, oppression, and bullying. A bit later in this section, we discuss the challenge of social media actually promoting inaction. Here, we will focus instead on other forms of digital media and how they can provide a platform for social action. This is not meant to be a primer for how to start a blog, podcast, or other digital media program, or the technical aspects of doing so. Instead, we focus on considerations if you are going to use digital media as a social action mechanism.

Because digital media is constantly evolving and changing, there are new blogs, vlogs, podcasts, websites, and other resources every day. Blogs are a common way individuals can present their perspectives on a timely topic, particularly one that is not represented elsewhere. Organizations have also incorporated blogs and blog series. An example of a blog series can be seen from the American Psychological Association titled *Psychology Benefits Society*. In this blog, authors apply psychological knowledge and research to current issues. Installment topics vary and include discussions such as the one on *Race, Racism, and Law Enforcement in Communities of Color* (https://psychologybenefits.org/race-and-law-enforcement/) and another on *Islamophobia in the U.S.* (https://psychologybenefits.org/2016/04/29/islamophobia-in-the-u-s-a-threat-to-justice-everywhere/), which address issues of individual and systemic oppression and the impact on people's lives and well-being. Further, organizations whose sole purpose is social change or advocacy around a particular issue often create and maintain blogs to share information, awareness, and inspire action.

There are a number of platforms for creating blogs and staying connected to social justice issues and activists such as Tumblr, WordPress, Wix, and others. Choosing a platform, theme, name, style, and format are all part of the creation process, and we recommend considering guidance from experienced bloggers and organizations. The Peace and Collaborative Development Network (PCDN) provides a great resource for creating and maintaining blogs focused on social issues (https://pcdnetwork.org/resources/guide-to-blogging-for-peace-and-social-change/). They have several suggestions for would-be bloggers: pick a topic that is timely and that you are passionate about; determine the audience you are trying to reach and understand the best way to reach them; read other blogs to see what you like and don't like about the way they approach the task; and choose a platform.

Oxfam also provides some blogging-related guidance oriented for NGOs (nongovernmental organizations) and individuals representing such organizations (https://oxfamblogs.org/fp2p/blogging-about-development-some-tips-for-ngos-and-would-be-bloggers/). If you are considering blogging on behalf of an organization, whether it is your employer or simply an organization in which you are engaged, this resource provides important considerations and suggestions.

Many organizations, such as media outlets, foundations, or advocacy groups, have great examples of podcasts that provide information, discussion, and resources regarding issues of concern. There are also excellent homegrown examples that take on tough issues, inspire conversation, and feature guests who are participating in activism. Some podcasts cover a wide range of issues, while others are linked more closely to issues related to a particular profession, group, or concern. Below is a list of some examples to check out (list compiled 12/2018).

These examples may provide you with inspiration as well as help you to think about how you can use this platform as a strategy to reach a social justice goal. As with all strategies, it is essential to have the overall goal as well as your sub-goals or strategies clearly articulated to help accomplish that goal. Then you can consider whether a podcast, or any other type of media strategy, may be a useful and effective approach to moving closer to that goal. In that process, do your homework: Is a podcast going to achieve that goal? What will your podcast do that isn't already being done? What

**TABLE 6.1**  Social Justice Related Podcasts

| NAME AND HOST | BRIEFLY ... |
| --- | --- |
| *Code Switch* by NPR with Gene Demby and Shareen Marisol Meraji | Conversations about race, ethnicity, and culture, and how it affects people's lived experiences |
| *Combat Jack* with Combat Jack and Dallas Penn | Hip hop-focused social justice conversations |
| *Edge of Sports* with Dave Zirin, sports editor for the *Nation* | Sports-focused social justice conversations |
| *Another Round* with Helen Nigatu and Tracy Clayton | Conversations focused on issues facing Black people and Black women in particular |
| *Intersection* with Jamil Smith, senior editor of the *New Republic* | Explores issues related to how various forms of oppression and discrimination are interlinked as well as how to address these together |
| *Backtalk* with Bitch Media editors Sarah Mirk and Amy Lam | Focuses on issues women face, news, the media, and social justice |
| *@TWiBPrime* with Elon James from #TeamBlackness | Politics, religion, and racial justice in the Black community |
| *Best of the Left* (collection) | Curated collection of podcasts available on the Internet that inform and guide around social action and activism issues |
| *Show about Race* with Baratunde Thurston, Raquel Cepeda, and Tanner Colby | Engaged dialogue around issues of race and racial justice |
| *Naming It* with Bedford Palmer and Lamisha Hill | Two Black psychologists "exploring the intersections of social justice, psychology, and Blackness" |
| *Social Justice League* with Love Lee and Seamus Kirst | Discusses current events and social justice work being done as well as actionable steps |
| *Service Roads: Conversations on Law and Social Justice* with Patrick Sellars, Logan Wexler & Eyad Saqr | Focuses on using the law for social change with guests such as lawyers, judges, formerly incarcerated community members, advocates, and others |
| *Do You Even Lift Bro? Men Exercising Social Justice* by Rocky Mountain Student Media | Explores how men can be better social justice advocates and how masculinity and other identities influence how men see the world and act or don't act |

technical expertise and equipment is necessary, and do you have access to that? If you decide a podcast is an important strategy, how can your podcast support and contribute to those already working on these issues? These and other questions are also relevant when considering other media projects such as those discussed later.

Developing a successful podcast is an art. Many social action or activism podcasts use an interview format as the core of their programming. Mac Prichard, a communications consultant for "social changemakers," provides tips for being a "great podcast interviewer" (https://www.prichardcommunications.com/10-ways-to-be-a-great-podcast-interviewer-2/). He emphasizes the importance of identifying ideal guests who have the expertise and experience you want and are good communicators. Then, he says, stick with your guidelines, and don't make exceptions simply out of convenience.

In addition to interviews and other content, podcast hosts provide context as well as connect and create lasting relationships with the audience to enhance continued commitment of the listeners. Storytelling is one of the strategies that can help. Christine Rose suggests elements that can help create a compelling narrative-style podcast (https://www.thepodcasthost.com/planning/7-storytelling-elements-improve-podcast/). First, focus on a central idea, and be clear about the reason for your story. Second, "create captivating characters," and provide the audience with an opportunity to feel like they know a little about the character (even you) so they develop an emotional connection to the character or storyteller (you). You may choose to use first-person ("I") or third person ("they") point of view, and tell the story from that perspective. Third, an engaging story has an element of conflict or drama between or within characters or in a situation experienced by the character. Fourth, creating an image of the setting can help immerse the audience in the story. The tone of your voice, the language, and the pace all contribute to feelings experienced by the audience whether it is urgency, meandering, wistful, angry, or dreamy.

There are a number of considerations when you choose to host a blog, podcast, or other digital resource. First, because these are serial products—in other words, provided in a series—there is a time commitment to producing them on a regular basis. Second, creating the blog or podcast is only the first step; ensuring that people know about it and follow it is as important as its existence in the first place. Publicity, marketing, and getting the word out may require a different set of skills than what you are used to. Go back to your assessment of your strengths and see where you excel now, what skills or knowledge you may need to develop, and consider who you can tap to bring in expertise that you don't already have.

Ethical and safety issues are critical when developing a public persona through digital media. Speaking out in your community makes your message visible both to people who agree with you and people who don't. When you use a digital platform, whether it be social media, websites, blogs, or others, your message goes far beyond the community you know and may stay out there permanently. Some of the considerations provided by Peace and Collaborative

Development Network are good to consider (https://pcdnetwork.org/resources/guide-to-blogging-for-peace-and-social-change/). First, there are safety issues such as potential consequences for your posts, including online or in-person attacks. In extreme situations, someone may object strongly enough to incite legal action; for example, if you say something about them personally. Second, think about who your voice is representing (intentionally or unintentionally), how you can appropriately represent an issue with integrity and solidarity (revisit the Solidarity chapter of this workbook), how you can moderate the assumptions made about whom you are "representing," and the possible consequences of what you say for the group you are "representing." Finally, ensure that you have permission if you are presenting material that you did not create.

Podcasts, blogs, and other platforms inspire action and inform you and the community in ways that are far-reaching. Remember that social action involves action, so make sure to move beyond listening and creating to actually doing! What is your goal in engaging with media as a consumer or creator? How will this actually make change?

## Implementing Change in Your Workplace or Your Profession

The strategies described above are largely framed as public action. Yet, making a difference in social issues can be a part of the way you approach your job, function within your organization, and help foster social justice through your work. Any occupation has the potential to present opportunities for social change. If you are considering how to address issues within your occupation, organization, or school, there are some strategies to consider, depending on your work context, your role, and elements of power.

### EXAMPLE

#### Muninder

As professors, both Rebecca and I work toward systemic change to try to make our workplace more socially just. I have worked within organizations on issues of Islamophobia, racism, and power differentials. For example, in our college, I worked with staff and faculty who were interested in addressing issues of race and racism. Together, we brought light to the ways in which racism is embedded in our system, and we were committed to enact change. We organized large-scale activities that engaged everyone and smaller-scale events that brought together smaller groups of stakeholders and administrators to address ways in which racism was problematizing certain processes. For example, we worked on issues related to Faculty of Color retention and differential rates of tenure and promotions compared to White faculty; faculty encountering racism regarding their research with racial and ethnic minority groups; and microaggressions against Women of Color staff.

Other examples can be seen where employees, either individually or as a group, bring injustice to the attention of their employer. Historically, labor unions have been one way this has happened. However, it can also happen outside that structure. For example, employees may band together to protest injustice when they feel like an issue is not being adequately addressed. In 2018, Google employees in offices around the world walked out to protest the way the company had handled sexual misconduct cases. Over 20,000 employees participated in the walkouts, and subsequently, there were a number of initiatives that the employee groups engaged in to demand responsiveness from their employer. In 2019, hundreds of employees from Facebook signed a letter to the company protesting policies that allow false political advertisements on the platform. Earlier in the year, Amazon employees planned a walkout demanding the company address the impact of practices on the environment. There are a range of ways to participate in social change from inside your workplace; some working within the system, some challenging the system. Engaging in activism and advocacy in your workplace can be a very important way to contribute to change yet can also be risky, depending on the situation. Toward the end of our discussion of strategies, we present some activities to help you think through ways to evaluate strategies as well as potential outcomes and consequences.

It is important to consider ways we can incorporate social change regardless of our job or workplace. It is also possible to find a job that will allow you to engage directly in social justice work. In terms of choosing a career path focused on social change, there are a number of ways to do this. You can choose a career path where you have the training to do the types of activism you feel is most aligned with your interests or skills, such as in media or community organizing. Alternatively, organizations that focus on activism and social change around issues such as the environment, education, and human rights all need different types of workers, jobs, and expertise to accomplish the organizations social justice goals (e.g., accountants, individuals in public relations, human resource professionals, writers, scientists, custodians, managers). If you want your paid job to involve activism, you can do that by using occupational training and experience you already have within an organization that is working on issues you care about or by getting training, experience, and education in careers and jobs that are activist roles. Or, you can work to make change within your organization.

## Everyday Actions

*Do one thing every day that scares you.*

—Eleanor Roosevelt

*Everyday Actions* are small things that we can do each day. Some take only minutes, some a little longer. These actions contribute to the big picture, the playbook, or just deal with unexpected issues that need some advocacy. They can bridge many of the issues we care about and provide an opportunity for us to live and demonstrate our commitment and values across the broad span of justice. They don't necessarily require much training or skill, just action, yet they are important when they are intentional and change oriented. A number of strategies described earlier in this workbook, such as contacting policy makers by phone or email about issues, can be everyday actions. There are also opportunities that arise unexpectedly and may be unwanted. For example, systemic oppression is built into structures that rule our lives (into policies, laws, school systems, health care, etc.) as well as individual acts of oppression, discrimination, and disrespect. The role you choose in visibly intervening or speaking up can make a big impact on those involved and help you act on what you believe. Opportunities for everyday action can show up in our personal life as well as our employment and can help move us toward more justice whether that be respect in the workplace, equity in opportunities, freedom from harassment, and other situations. One of the essential assumptions about everyday action is that it is in everyone's best interest to intervene or disrupt oppression and injustice, not just the person who is the target of injustice.

There are three parts of everyday action: awareness, information or knowledge, and action. Awareness refers to recognizing when something has happened that is unjust and where we are in relation to the injustice. What experiences have we had in the past that shape how we perceive or experience this situation? What biases might we hold about the situation or people involved? What feelings do we have about intervening? How does our own experience or our own biases influence our understanding of the situation? Understanding the dynamics raised by these questions is an important prerequisite for preparing yourself to engage in everyday action. The section on positionality in the Solidarity chapter of this workbook can be useful to help you examine your position in these situations.

People who are not targets of oppression toward a specific group may have trouble recognizing that injustice when it happens. They may need to be more intentional, noticing interactions and situations through a lens of privilege and oppression. A very basic example is that, as a person who is able to walk, I (Rebecca) don't always notice barriers for people who use wheelchairs or crutches. As a White person, I typically don't experience being ignored by retail clerks based on my skin color. Because I have worked on increasing my racial awareness, my ability to notice when another customer with darker skin is ignored has increased but there are still times I don't catch it. When I do notice it, my interpretation of that event and my choice to act is often shaped more by the immediate circumstances and my values rather than by personal experiences of oppression. On the other hand, people who are targets of oppression may be aware of that oppression frequently. As a Person of Color, I (Muninder) am constantly aware of the impact of race in settings I am in and I am aware when someone is treated differently based on skin color. The choice whether to respond, and how, is affected by a number of things, such as what just happened; whether it was intentional or unintentional; how much energy is needed to address the issue; whether there is a clear way to address it; whether addressing it will actually help; what the costs are if I address it (for others and for myself); and other considerations. For people who experience injustice regularly, intervening can be complicated and tiring. Having to choose daily, or hourly, whether or not to confront someone, whether to try to educate someone, or even whether to listen openly to someone who disagrees, can require a lot of energy. When injustice is personal to our lives, it can feel like a personal attack, and sometimes it is. For example, as a child of immigrants and someone who has many family and community members who are immigrants, for me, a verbal attack on immigrants who are citizens, green card holders, undocumented immigrants, or narratives about deportation can feel like a personal threat. It can feel hard to act, and I can even feel paralyzed into inaction.

It is also important to note that just because we recognize one type of oppression or injustice doesn't mean we will recognize another type. For example, we may notice racist behavior but not sexist behavior. In addition, injustice that comes from an individual (for example, a racist comment) may be easier to recognize than systemic or broader-scale injustices (such as discrimination in housing loan rates) because those may be more subtle and built into policies or practices. Thus, someone who is "just following the policy" may be acting with injustice, but it may not be as easy to see. Recognizing system level injustice is more likely when we understand the context of this specific circumstance as well as the historical and sociopolitical backdrop that may shape what is happening now and how that contributes to the harm that is being done.

The second part of everyday action is knowledge or information about the situation, including background or history, the immediate context, and possible outcomes. How much do you know about what is happening? What is the historical context for what is happening now? Who is involved, directly or indirectly? How much do you need to know? Information comes from observation as well as educating yourself about the types of situations that you may encounter. Knowing the people who live and work around us and the issues they face can provide a context when issues come up. Grounding ourselves in a commitment to humanity and using our observations and knowledge to act on that commitment can help intervene in unjust systems. For example, if we live in a community that includes recent immigrants, it would be helpful to develop relationships with people in our community who have experience as immigrants. It would also be helpful to learn about actions that Immigrations Customs Enforcement (ICE) may take in communities like ours and to know the rights of people who encounter ICE. If we are not likely to be targeted by ICE personally, it is also helpful to know our rights as witnesses and supports for our community members. This knowledge would help us provide assistance and advocate for members of our community if they have an encounter with ICE.

The awareness we develop and the knowledge and information we gain can lead to us to become more effective in the third part of everyday action, intervention. What would we do in an actual situation? How can we intervene and follow up? The work by Derald Wing Sue and his colleagues on microaggressions (Sue, 2010) and microinterventions (Sue, Alsaidi, Awad, Glaeser, Calle, & Mendez, 2019) can be really useful in recognizing these oppressions as well as ideas about how to intervene. In the next section, we explore various ways to engage when we witness acts of injustice.

## Intervening in Individual Acts of Injustice

There are so many daily acts of injustice that we can't possibly address them all here. We will, however, mention a few examples and suggest some ideas for action as well as provide some resources and encourage you to learn more. Individual acts of injustice include such things as exclusion from services, mistreatment, harassment, hostile or derogatory language or behavior (including "humor"), and other examples where someone with dominant privilege uses their power over another in an unjust way. Microaggression and related terms are used when the act is subtle (such as ignoring or making stereotypical assumptions based on race, gender, disability, or other identities). When actions are more visible and clearer (such as racial slurs), we name it as overt hostility and harassment. The impact of these individual acts of injustice is often shaped by the extent to which you are the target, experience with this type of aggression, the power and relationship with the person perpetuating the aggression, and the intent of the behavior.

## Microaggressions

The term "microaggression" was proposed in 1970 by Chester Pierce (see the work of Pierce and his colleagues published in 1978) to describe dismissals and insults toward Black Americans from others. In 2007, Derald Wing Sue and his colleagues, psychologists, and scholars of microaggressions, described three types of microaggressions, including microassaults (conscious and intentional verbal or physical actions such as slurs, aggressive acts, etc.), microinsults (rudeness or insensitivity based on race, ethnicity, gender or other identity), and microinvalidations (actions that exclude, ignore, or invalidate based on race, ethnicity, or other identity). They describe microinsults and microinvalidations as more subtle and thus more difficult to identify and suggest that this may leave the person receiving the microaggression to question what just happened, whether it was related to their identity, and whether they should respond. Similarly, for someone who is in the presence of a microaggression but is not the target, it may not be clear that something harmful has just happened and the extent of the harm caused. With microaggressions, the intent does not necessarily match the impact. In other words, whether the person who commits the microaggression intended it or not, the impact is often still harmful.

### EXAMPLE

### Microaggression and Microintervention

The following example reflects a microaggression likely stemming from unconscious bias. A group enters a restaurant (a man in a wheelchair and two women and one man who are standing), and the host immediately talks directly to the standing male customer to inquire if they'd like a table. It is very likely that the host has assumed that the man without a disability is in charge and more capable of answering than the others in the party. We draw this conclusion given the history of power in the U.S., specifically that men without visible disabilities have been assumed to be "in charge" and/or more capable than people with disabilities and women. For the customer in the wheelchair and the women customers, the extent of harm will be affected by a number of factors, such as how often they have experienced being treated as invisible or "less than" others who have more able-bodied privilege or gender privilege, as well the circumstance (for example, if the standing man is actually the boss). In our example, if the man in the wheelchair is actually the one making the reservation, he could interrupt and answer the host. Alternatively, the standing man, when addressed by the host, could redirect the host's attention to the man in the wheelchair by saying something to the effect of "my colleague here is in charge of the reservations." That would be a subtle way of redirecting the host's action at the time. In addition, if using this as a learning opportunity, one of the members of the party could talk with the host and point out the possible assumption communicated and hopefully make a more lasting change.

Sue and his colleagues provide guidance in the form of microinterventions, or strategies that we might use when encountering microaggressions (see Sue, Alsaidi, Awad, Glaeser, Calle, & Mendez, 2019). They suggest four types of strategies: "make the invisible visible" (e.g., name the observation of the biased behavior), "disarm the microaggression/macroaggression" (e.g., disagree with the biased statement), "educate the offender" (e.g., provide information that explains why the statement or behavior was offensive), and "seek external intervention" (e.g., reach out to others for support or intervention) (see the article by Sue and his colleagues in *American Psychologist*, 2019). There are a few resources that illustrate how these interventions can be done. For example, in the mid-2000s, the National Underground Railroad Freedom Center produced a series of short public service announcements, "The Power of One," providing scenarios which illustrated people speaking up in very small ways that disrupted and called attention to an interpersonal injustice, usually involving microaggressions (https://www.youtube.com/watch?v=WlT8I04JYIk). The videos featured situations in which a person observed someone, often a friend or colleague, demonstrating racist and anti-Semitic behaviors and then responded expressing disagreement, disapproval, disappointment, or educating the person who was offensive. Many of these examples reflect the strategies described by Sue and his colleagues. Another good source is "Did you really just say that?," a short article provided by the American Psychological Association (https://www.apa.org/monitor/2017/01/microaggressions). There are other resources available and opportunities online to examine and practice recognizing and intervening with microaggressions. We recommend spending some time exploring these as well as considering the following activities.

Addressing microaggressions effectively, especially if you are not the target in the situation, is an important form of everyday action, and yet some of us may need practice. In this next activity, consider how you would respond in situations where microaggressions occur.

ACTIVITY 6.14

## What Would You Do?

Choose one of the two scenarios below (preferably one in which you hold sociopolitical privilege in race, gender, ability status, religion, etc.). Reflect on the situation and circumstances, then determine how you might respond.

*Scenario 1*: *You are on a bus and notice that a young Man of Color gets on the bus followed by a young White man (they are traveling separately). A White passenger sitting in the seat in front of you clearly blocks the seat beside him when the Man of Color approaches then opens it when the White passenger approaches. It is clear that they do not know each other.*

*Scenario 2*: *You are eating your lunch in a public park around noon and notice that there is a man kneeling on a carpet in prayer. There are two older women sitting on a park bench nearby talking loudly about the man saying things like, "that's just not appropriate here," "that should be done in private," "this is a public park," etc.*

Choose one of the above scenarios, and consider the following questions:

1. What is the situation, and what are possible microaggressions happening?
2. What is your cultural positionality in relation to the people who are being aggressive and in relation to the person who is the target of their aggression?
3. What are possible behaviors you could engage in to intervene?
4. Is it possible or desirable to check in with the person who is the target to find out if they would like you to intervene? How might you do it?
5. Are there real safety issues involved for you or for the person who is the target of the microaggression?
6. How might you follow up? In other words, is there something you can do in your community to reduce the likelihood of this type of thing happening in the future?

The above examples are just a few situations that may contain microaggressions. For some of us, these may seem familiar, given the communities we live in. For others, the types of microaggressions that come up may look different. One of the challenges of microaggressions is their subtlety for people who are not the target. Further, to notice them, we need to be paying attention. With increasing preoccupation with smartphones, there seem to be a lot more people who go through their day without engaging or paying attention to what is going on in the world around them.

The next activity is designed to explore the microaggressions you see in your own community.

## Becoming and Being Observant

### Part 1: Becoming and Being Observant in Your Own Community

Over the next few days, intentionally observe interactions in your community (e.g., on the bus, on the street, in shops, in restaurants) and notice interactions that occur between people who share different identities. In particular, notice interactions between people who hold privileged status in relation to another.

You may be very aware of microaggressions that are directed toward you, but for this exercise, we are asking you to pay attention to microaggressions directed toward others. Just a few examples of microaggressions might include someone not giving up a seat on a bus to a passenger with a disability, a clerk or host serving a White or male customer before an Asian customer or a woman who had been waiting first, someone clutching their bag or phone more tightly when a Man of Color passes, someone touching a Black woman's hair, and many others. The commonality between these examples is that there are stereotypes or power dynamics that are reinforced in a way that ignores, harms, or communicates a subtle message that the person of a marginalized or targeted identity is not wanted, is dangerous, is less important, or is otherwise demeaned.

Record your observations, including: Who was involved? What was the context? Did it seem intentional or unintentional? How did the person targeted seem to react? Would intervention be helpful? How? What might you do if you were to intervene? How does your positionality (your relationship and history with privilege and oppression) shape the way you interpret the answers to these questions?

### Part 2: Being Observant of Yourself

For the second part of the exercise, pay attention to your own activities, and in particular, notice your behaviors, thoughts, and emotions. When you are engaging with others and you have a position of privilege, are there things you do that communicate that you have more power? Are there things you do that perpetuate or act out stereotypes? What do you do when you realize that you have exerted your power or acted on a bias?

In the light of the historical reality of sexual harassment and women being at greater risk of sexual assault by men, there is a real need for women to be attentive to their safety. Sometimes, our behavior is protective and learned over time for survival. As women, we may be more cautious around men, especially men we don't know. At the same time, we also have to pay attention to when unfair biases might be influencing the way we see things and our behavior because of messages we have learned from family, society, and the media. We have been raised to pay attention and be skeptical of men for our own protection, regardless of their skin color. Further, because of the context of historical (and current) racism in the United States, White women have been socialized to fear Men of Color, especially darker-skinned men, more so than others with no evidence that Men of Color are inherently more dangerous than White men. The messages about who is safe and unsafe often is incorporated into the way we see and move in the world. To take everyday social action in the presence of microaggressions and discrimination, we need to first look at ourselves.

## Overt Hostility and Harassment

Whether and how we take everyday action in the face of overt hostility and harassment depends on the circumstances and our resources. For example, is it you or someone else being harassed? Who is doing the harassing (e.g., a member of the general public or an official)? What kinds of resources are available (e.g., who, if anyone, is allied with you; do you have a phone, etc.)? We will touch on just a couple of these and note resources that can provide you with additional useful information.

If you are the target of overt hostility and harassment, there are a number of reactions you might have, depending on the type of mistreatment, what the aggression is targeting (e.g., racial hostility, hostility due to action you have taken, etc.), the danger, who is the aggressor, the likelihood of harm, whether your family is threatened, whether you feel like you have support from others, whether you can trust security resources (e.g., police), and other variables. These vary so much, depending on the situation, that we won't be able to address them fully. Fortunately, there are great resources and communities that provide more specific guidance and support. For example, Black Lives Matter shares a beautiful *Healing Action Toolkit* that acknowledges and integrates healing work with activism strategies within a framework of liberation, traditions, and historical trauma (https://blacklivesmatter.com/resource/healing-justice-toolkit/). The earlier section on Solidarity noted the power of numbers and finding support in camaraderie. In addition to the multitude of voices that come from larger numbers, there is also a greater likelihood that you will be able to learn from people who have survived harassment and hostility. The lessons they have learned can provide support, encouragement, insight, and inspiration.

There are a few points we will mention that may be helpful across circumstances for people targeted by hate and hostility. First, make sure you and your family are safe to the extent that you decide is necessary. Second, reach out to others who have had similar experiences and/or who will be supportive. Sometimes this can be done locally, other times it may mean reaching beyond your geographic community. It may not even mean sharing what happened to you but at least finding people who validate and acknowledge the wrongness of what happened. If you are able to share what happened (or continues to happen), acting as a group to call out the aggressor may feel safer and make the voice louder. Help others know what would be most helpful to you. Third, investigate your rights and avenues for pursuing your rights. Legal avenues can be costly in many ways, but they can also be very useful, depending on the situation, whether it is a restraining order or a civil lawsuit. Investigate the options available to you for legal counsel, if appropriate, and determine whether this avenue will accomplish your goals. There are advocacy organizations that may be able to provide helpful legal advice or support depending on the situation; some national organizations include Southern Poverty Law Center, NAACP, MALDEF, and others. You may find local organizations as well that can be helpful.

If you are an observer of someone being targeted, you have choices about how to respond either by intervening or witnessing. It is important that this choice is made thoughtfully with awareness of the situation, and the wishes of the person being targeted so you know the level of danger, appropriateness of various alternatives, and choose whether and how to become involved. Thinking through how you might respond ahead of time, before situations arise, allows you to think more clearly and act more quickly when you are in the situation. It also gives you time to seek some training ahead of time that will help you respond more effectively if a situation arises.

### EXAMPLE

## Rebecca

I know that as a smallish, White, middle-aged woman, in certain situations, I may have advantages. I may appear to be relatively nonthreatening to other White people or to those in positions of power. This may help if I am working to de-escalate a hostile situation. On the other hand, I am vulnerable to violence because I am small and subject to gendered violence because I am a woman. I also have two children, and it is important to me to be safe, if at all possible, so I can care for them. Therefore, I have sought training for self-defense, de-escalation, and witnessing, and have made a conscious decision to use intervention tactics that will be less likely to put me directly in the line of violence. I also recognize that my racial and economic privilege allows me to make these choices. Because I am a White, middle-aged woman and economically middle class, I am less likely to be the target of hostility and violence in most situations in my life. Thus, it is important for me to be willing to intervene as a witness or an accomplice, using strategies that are described below.

Intervening as an accomplice or witness involves engaging in a harassment situation with the intent of supporting the person being harassed, helping preserve their safety as well as your own, and acting on values that harassment is not acceptable. There are a number of great resources to help us think through and prepare to intervene as bystanders, accomplices, or witnesses. Hollaback, a "global, people-powered movement to end harassment," provides online training and guidance and describes five methods for supporting someone who is being targeted with physical or verbal threats: direct, distract, delegate, delay, and document (https://www.ihollaback.org/resources/bystander-resources/). Reflecting on the following questions can help determine the best approach, although the answers may not always be clear. What are the safety issues for you and for the person who is targeted? Does the person targeted want someone to speak for them? How likely is it that the situation will escalate? Hollaback suggests that direct intervention is the most risky yet sometimes is appropriate. *Direct intervention* is the act of calling out what you are observing as unacceptable. Hollaback suggests that your statements should be short (e.g., "that's inappropriate") and should not engage in debate or discussion as that is likely to escalate the situation. *Distract*, a second method, aims to interrupt the situation and ally with the person being targeted in a subtle way. In this strategy, in the midst of the harassment, you engage with the person being targeted in an unrelated way not directly addressing the harassment. For example, if you witness someone on a bus being harassed verbally by another passenger, you might consider sitting next to the targeted person and do nothing but sit there and make eye contact with them indicating that you are a friendly companion. Or you might pretend that you are lost and ask for directions. Although this strategy is generally safer than directly confronting the aggressor, there are still some safety considerations, and it is important not to exacerbate concerns that the targeted person may be feeling. *Delegation* involves asking for help from a third party. In this scenario, you could alert the bus driver to the situation or engage other passengers as helpers. If you are traveling with a friend, working together can be helpful, with one of you causing a distraction and the other one checking in with the person being targeted. Calling police can be a complicated choice given the history of police response in that community, the people involved, and the training of the police (are they focused and trained in de-escalation or force?). Further, it is important to check in with the targeted person first to make sure that is what they would want. The goal is to de-escalate the situation and remove the potential for harm. Sometimes when force is met by force, the situation can escalate. Further, if the police in that area have a history of acting in a way that does not de-escalate or tends to criminalize people from particular groups, then it may be good to consider other alternatives. *Delay* is the fourth tactic described by Hollaback, suggesting that it is helpful to follow up with the targeted person after the event, even if you did not intervene while it was occurring. Finally, *Documenting* what you observe is important in a number of ways. There are guidelines for intervening that can be reviewed and practiced, maximizing the rights of the person being harassed, the effectiveness of your efforts, and your safety and the safety of others. Some examples of guidelines and bystander training include: Hollaback (https://www.ihollaback.org/guide-bystander-intervention/), Southern Poverty Law Center (https://www.splcenter.org/20171005/splc-campus-guide-bystander-intervention), Human Rights Defenders (https://www.newtactics.org/staying-safe-security-resources-human-rights-defenders/staying-safe-security-resources-human-rights), the American Friends Service Committee (https://www.afsc.org/resource/dos-and-donts-bystander-intervention), and Resolution Northwest (https://resolutionsnorthwest.org/resources/).

Social media has increased public recording, posting, and viewing of violence, harassment, and bias on the part of police, security, and other "enforcers," with some videos going viral. Although this allows more people to see these videos and may help to spread awareness of violence against communities, it does not necessarily result in a coordinated response to support the community or challenge unjust actions. With increased attention to examples of police and other public officials engaging in harassment or unnecessary force, there are more organizations that provide guidance and resources for reporting, witnessing, and documenting. Organizations such as CopWatch (https://www.berkeleycopwatch.org; http://wecopwatch.org) provide trainings about community members' rights, how to safely be an effective observer and witness, and how to document what you see.

Because of the increase in access and enhanced use of cellphones, there are also tools that have been developed where users can actually report immediately to organizations that will take the footage and documentation and act on it to advocate for justice. For example, the ACLU created a cell phone app, Mobile Justice CA, to provide cell phone carriers with a way to record and immediately report interactions with law enforcement to local ACLU representatives. The advantage of immediate reporting, in addition to the potential for larger-scale advocacy, is that the record of the incident is no longer only held on an individual's cell phone, vulnerable if the phone is seized. There is also a "witness" feature in the app that provides information about incidents that may be occurring in your area. This feature is especially helpful for community groups to work more closely together to monitor law enforcement. There is a third function, "alerts," that provides information about local and statewide ACLU events. In addition to monitoring community policing, airport security is another area where individuals have found a way to respond to bias and incidents of harassment. FlyRights, an app developed by the Sikh Coalition in 2012, allows travelers to complete a brief survey and report incidents they experience in which they feel unfairly profiled while traveling, especially in encounters with airport security. These reports are automatically sent as official complaints directly to the TSA.

## Online Harassment and Aggression

Online harassment is increasingly problematic given our use of social media. According to a 2017 study by the Pew Research Center, 66% of U.S. adults have observed harassing behavior toward others online, and 40% reported being the target of online hostility (http://www.pewinternet. org/2017/07/11/witnessing-online-harassment/). In a follow-up article, researchers presented different scenarios to learn what types of behaviors were perceived as harassing and found a range of interpretations in scenarios involving elements of sexism and racism (http://www.pewinternet. org/2018/01/04/crossing-the-line-what-counts-as-online-harassment/). The American Bar Association states that this type of harassment and bullying is difficult to address, particularly because law enforcement has limited understanding of this as a problem and may minimize it. Further, because laws are generally state specific but online activity is global, there is often a lack of concrete legal action available. Still, there is increased discussion over the past couple of years about the responsibility of online providers to respond to hateful or harmful online activity. This has yet to be resolved, and the tension between free speech, censorship, and harassment has created a complex tangle resulting in very little clarity or action. Getting involved in these discussions or holding social media companies accountable could be potential outlets for your social action.

Ashe Dryden, who writes on diversity in the technology sector, reports that she is targeted regularly online given her status as a woman in a male-dominated field and provides some guidance for people who also face this type of hostility (https://www.ashedryden.com/blog/you-asked-how-do-i-deal-with-online-harassment-how-do-i-help-the-targets-of-online-harassment). First, she suggests contacting people who are close to you to let them know what is going on. If you become a target because of your work, activism, public statements, or other online activity, harassers may try to spread their efforts to others. Informing those people about what is going on can help them act if they become a target. Ashe also provides specific guidance for people who want to help when they see others being harassed online, such as what to include or not include in responses, cautions about posting information, and other great tips. She also provides additional technical suggestions for people who are targeted, including blocking senders, considering "blocking bots," regularly revisiting privacy settings, and other strategies.

Dryden acknowledges that online harassment creates a tremendous amount of stress, exhaustion, and sometimes fear, and emphasizes the importance of taking care of yourself and talking with others you trust for support. Dryden receives threats and harassment so regularly that people have reached out and asked how to help. Because the threats can be exhausting and recounting them and directing others can add to that exhaustion, she began posting suggestions of what she would like from others who want to help. That way, she doesn't need to repeatedly respond directly to each person, but allies can still access the information and act. The Sustainability section of this workbook focuses on just that: developing a plan to help keep you healthy, energized, and balanced.

## Talking with People We Don't Necessarily Agree With

There are a number of different types of situations where opportunities arise to engage in conversations about topics with people who have views different from our own: our family, our community, our workplace, and others. The context we are in, what experiences we have, how prepared and intentional we are in the moment, and our goal for having the conversation may all affect how we engage. Our positions and appearance as women, a Woman of Color and a White woman, shape the way people approach us and shape the way we have conversations about racism.

**EXAMPLE**

## Muninder

As a Woman of Color, I do not often seek out conversations with people who challenge an initiative I support, but many times, my appearance, my dress, and my name are strong enough triggers that unwittingly solicit an invitation to a conversation (often unwanted) as I live out my normal day. I am often prepared with responses because the initiatives I engage in are tied to my own lived experiences or the lived experiences of loved ones. For example, at a university fundraiser event for student scholarships with predominantly White individuals in attendance, I am hyperconscious that when I introduce myself (my name and my profession), the outfit I chose to wear, or the fact that I am not White can all be interpreted as an invitation to discuss topics as varied as immigration, culture, gender roles, discrimination and racism, and even social justice. What might begin as an educational statement about Indians or Sikhs or People of Color can rapidly move into a discussion of current events, politics, and legislation. I know I have to be "on" in dominant culture public domains. There are times when I choose to engage in the conversation and there are times when I try to end it rather quickly. This is often determined by a few factors, including how many internal resources I have at that time (e.g., how tired am I?), whether anyone might be emotionally harmed by my engagement in the conversation or lack thereof (e.g., allying with someone), whether I feel like having the conversation will make a difference, and how much time I have already allocated to these types of conversations.

**EXAMPLE**

## Rebecca

As a White woman, I engage in racial conversations intentionally and unintentionally (there are also many times when I choose not to engage). For example, I may choose to staff a table for United Against Hate (an initiative of one of the community organizations I belong to). Prior to that event, I mentally prepare myself for conversations that will be supportive of the initiative as well as those that might be against the organization and its activities. Because I enter this activity with intentionality, I am better able to center myself in the purpose (i.e., to facilitate dialogue around racist and hateful incidents in our community and actions to try to bring people together). Thus, I am better able to articulate and de-escalate if the person I am talking to becomes agitated and combative. Conversely, if I am attending a social event, I am less likely than Muninder to be perceived as inviting conversations about race, immigration, and other such topics simply given how I look. Still, in social situations, if someone begins a conversation with me denying racism or some other oppression issue, I may be taken off guard. I may jump into the conversation and try to balance sounding too academic, too argumentative, or too self-righteous with compassionately trying to hold the other person accountable. Or I may be tired and not want to engage with them about this topic at all. I may need to maintain a positive relationship with them (e.g., family, coworkers, etc.) and thus struggle to figure out how to address their comments and still maintain a positive relationship. As a White woman, I am very aware that I often am able to choose whether or not to engage in those conversations. When trying to decide whether I will invest the time and energy to have a meaningful dialogue with someone I may not agree with, I first think about why I am having the dialogue and the likelihood that it will be productive. If someone vehemently disagrees with me and is only interested in convincing me that they are right, I may choose not to engage or may end the conversation, unless I believe someone is being harmed.

Dylan Marron presents an interesting exploration of the way he has chosen to engage people who have expressed hostility against him. In his podcast, *Conversations with People Who Hate Me*, Dylan Marron contacts people who have written hateful messages to him through Twitter and other online forums and arranges phone calls and direct conversations to ask them why they felt compelled to say such hateful things (http://www.dylanmarron.com/podcast/). Each of us chooses a way to approach these types of challenges based on many factors, including our personality, culture, safety, skills, resources, and context. We provide some questions below that could be helpful when considering your approach.

## SUMMARY OF CONSIDERATIONS FOR HAVING TOUGH CONVERSATIONS:

1. Does this person want to have a conversation, or do they want to argue? If you get the sense they are interested in dialogue, it will be more fruitful than if they are looking for an argument. Asking yourself the same question can also be good.
2. Do you want to have the conversation? Do you have a choice? When I (Muninder) see someone being treated disrespectfully due to their racial or ethnic background by employees of a store, I speak to the employee and manager. I don't necessarily want to have that conversation, but I feel I do not have a choice.

3. What is the situation or context (what, where, who)? It is helpful to consider your identities and the identities of the person you are speaking to and the ways they might impact the interaction. For example, I (Rebecca) have more racial privilege and thus responsibility to speak out against racism than Muninder, who has a targeted identity as a Person of Color. In addition, context may include where and how the conversation comes up.

4. Do you feel physically, mentally, and emotionally prepared to engage in this conversation? There are times when we have the internal resources to have a conversation and there are others when we don't. It is helpful to consider your desire or ability to engage at that time.

5. Is it a safe context to have the conversation? If it doesn't feel psychologically or physically safe, is there a way to create more safety (e.g., gather allies, choose a different time and place)?

6. What is your goal (e.g., understand them, persuade them, learn from them, be understood by them, tell your story, run interference)? Knowing your goal will help you decide on how you want to engage. For example, if a grocery store employee yells in staccato English to a Spanish-speaking customer, our goal in intervening is to assist the customer and educate the employee, and possibly their manager, on how to better provide services to all of their customers.

7. What are the possible outcomes? What consequences might there be for you engaging in a conversation (e.g., impact on job stability, are bystanders impacted)? Knowing the possible outcomes may determine whether and how you engage and also prepares you to better deal with potential fallout.

There are some general strategies that can be helpful to guide you when engaging in these types of conversations. Principles discussed earlier in this workbook such as being clear about your message and having stories and examples that illustrate your perspective can help you to articulate your concerns. Understanding the motivations and feelings of the person you are talking to can also help you to have patience and openness to listening.

While in conversation with people we disagree with, there is often the possibility that we may become agitated, irritated, and triggered. These emotions are important to pay attention to as they may help us know when to leave the conversation or to take a breath. Staying clear and focused as well as managing our own emotions and safety are essential. Knowing our triggers and what helps us to stay calm is as essential as having a well-thought-out elevator speech.

## Rebecca

I know that I get triggered and feel frustrated when I feel like someone is patronizing me or refusing to listen to what I have to say. I am aware that as a White person, how I look and what I represent often allows me to talk with other White people and use that Whiteness in the conversation. It also shapes how and whether I choose to engage, or stay engaged, in a difficult dialogue with someone. When I am in a dialogue and find myself triggered, I have found a few phrases that work for me. If I feel it is important (and physically safe) to stay in the dialogue, I repeat things like "I would like to talk with you, but in order to do that I need you to _____ (e.g., provide concrete examples of what you mean: lower your voice, be willing to listen to what I have to say, consider that there is an alternate possibility)." If I am too tired, too frustrated, or feel unsafe, I say something like "I'm not sure we are getting anywhere," "I don't have the energy to have this conversation with you right now," or something along those lines to exit the conversation.

There are a number of great resources encouraging and facilitating people in reaching across political and social differences that provide specific strategies to use in such conversations. Examples of resources include the National Conversation Project (https://www.nationalconversationproject.org), Beyond the Bubble (https://www.facebook.com/BeyondtheBubbleDialogue/), Conversation Cafes (http://www.conversationcafe.org), the Listen First Project (http://www.listenfirstproject.org/essay-series/), the Center for Nonviolent Communication (https://www.cnvc.org), and others.

Having guidelines and resources can help in knowing when and how effective dialogue can happen. In the activity below, you will prepare to practice dialogue with someone you may not agree with. It is important to be mindful to choose a situation in which you feel relatively safe emotionally and physically for this activity. Below, consider what has stopped you from engaging in a conversation and how you could engage if you were to do things differently.

## Practicing Listening and Dialogue

**Part 1:** Consider a recent situation where you chose not to engage in a conversation with someone who disagreed with you about a social justice issue.

What stopped you from engaging?

_____

_____

_____

**Part 2:** Now, go back and read the Summary of Considerations for Having a Tough Conversation on the previous pages. Reflect on each of the seven considerations for this specific situation.

1.

2.

3.

4.

5.

6.

7.

**Part 3:** As you reflect on this situation, if you were to engage in a similar conversation in the future, what tools or preparation could help you feel more prepared?

_____

_____

_____

Engaging in conversations with those who don't agree with you can be a good way to build bridges, to understand another perspective, or to gain information that can help you and your allies consider strategies that might be needed for social change. Conversations require social interaction, whereas the next several strategies can be done with others, or completely on your own.

## Your Power as a Consumer: Boycotting and/or Divesting

Some very basic ways of taking action include being thoughtful and intentional about how we use our money, what we buy, where we spend, what services we pay for, and whom we support through our actions. Economic power as a consumer can be an important form of everyday action. In fact, boycotting and divesting as social action strategies have been shown to disrupt a company's business in many cases and can threaten their reputation, resulting in important consequences for their business. McDonnell and Werner studied how social action impacted business and shared the results of their study in *Administrative Science Quarterly* (2016). They summarized that such action actually did disrupt corporate political activity and explained:

> activists' challenges also disrupt their targets' financial market position and social management process, prompting downgrades by analysts (Vasi and King, 2012), spurring divestment by investors (Soule, 2009; Soule, Swaminathan, and Tihanyi, 2014), and threatening a firm's public image and reputation (King, 2008; McDonnell and King, 2013). (p. 586)

Yet, they found that the impact varies, depending on the characteristics of the business as well as how effectively the boycotting or divestment movement mobilizes and engages consumers.

For some of us, there are many choices in where we shop, how much we buy, and where we bank and invest. For others, part of the injustice lies in that we don't have as many choices economically or practically. Being informed about the companies, stores, or banks we do business with can help us responsibly decide among the choices we have. Some of these choices may involve not supporting certain businesses, not buying more than what we need, choosing certain products over others, or making our feelings known to the business.

## EXAMPLE

### Rebecca

Save West Berkeley Shellmound is an effort of an Indigenous-led group locally that is working to preserve sacred Shellmound land at risk of being developed into a shopping mall (https://shellmound.org). Nearby, other sacred land has already been turned into high-end shopping malls despite years of protesting. In addition to fighting development plans for undeveloped Shellmound land, every year on Black Friday, the group goes out to the shopping mall that is built on Indigenous Shellmounds for ceremony and raises awareness of shoppers with signs and flyers explaining that the mall is on sacred land. Most of the shoppers have no idea about the history of that area. Some ignore us, some actually thank us and say they will make a choice not to shop there. I am able to choose to not shop there, and I am able to distribute information with the group to discourage other shoppers.

Much further from my home, the protests at Standing Rock and the Dakota Access Pipeline (DAPL) also help to illuminate the large number of businesses, corporations, and financial services that are investing in the oil pipeline that is threatening land and treaties under the umbrella of an organization called Energy Transfer Partners. The Standing Rock Sioux tribe—as well as other tribes, environmental groups, and thousands of other supporters—have been trying to protect the water sources from the environmental dangers, including pipeline ruptures spilling oil on the land and in rivers. A number of organizations have shared information regarding the corporations and businesses that invested in the pipeline. Alternatively, other stakeholders and companies have communicated their support for the Standing Rock tribe and against the pipeline (see report from the Interfaith Center on Corporate Responsibility: https://www.iccr.org/investors-standing-standing-rock-sioux). With this information, I make choices about my personal business. For example, I have canceled certain credit cards, ensured that the credit union I use does not invest in oil, and made other decisions in an effort to be more socially responsible with regard to this issue in particular.

When we make choices as a consumer, it is important to communicate to the companies that we have made this choice, either to support or boycott, and why. Boycotting without communicating doesn't send a message and thus doesn't serve as action. Research by McDonnell and Werner (2016) showed that this action not only sends a message to the business, it can also potentially influence the political clout a corporation can have. Specifically, it may affect the willingness of politicians to associate with that business if they think it will affect their constituents' voting choices. It is important to note that this research was done in 2016, and the political climate has shifted toward pro-business policies, so many things are unclear. It is also important to note that on the flip side of boycotting, we can take action by supporting businesses that show a commitment to the issues that we care about.

In Activity 6.17, think about what guides you in considering how and where you spend your money.

**ACTIVITY 6.17**

### Investigating and Creating Your Consumer Guidelines

In this activity, you will take stock of where you spend your money and how that fits with your values. We all have choices, some of us more than others, to shift what businesses we support, what we expect from these businesses, and whether we really need those products or services. This is a pretty extensive activity if you do it fully so you may choose to focus on a little at a time, perhaps starting with the businesses you use most. As you read the questions below, use the table at the end to summarize your responses. Some of these questions may be tough to answer without a little research so feel free to get started, do some research, then come back and fill it in little by little.

**Part 1: Taking Stock**

1. What businesses do you support (e.g., bank, grocery, discount or department store, clothing, online shopping, gas, restaurants, investments, etc.)?
2. What conscious choices have you made already that are aligned with your values?

**Part 2: Investigating Whom You Support**

1. For each of the businesses you use regularly, find out what you can about how they reflect the values you think are important. For example, how well do they pay and support their workers? Do they contribute to the local community? How does their business affect the environment? What are their policies regarding hiring employees or serving customers (e.g., anti-LGBT, history of civil rights complaints, etc.)? What organizations or lobbying groups do they give money to? *Hint: We've found that using search terms such as "social responsibility," "protesting," "civil rights," and "carbon footprint" in Internet searches can expose news articles, civil rights or Equal Opportunity Employment complaints filed, etc. You can also get to know employees that work there; how do they feel they are treated by the company? Look for job postings and find out how much they pay and what the benefits are, if any. For "gig economy" work (e.g., Uber, Lyft, Task Rabbit, etc.), you can directly ask the workers what it is like to work for the company.*
2. For businesses whose practices or policies are not aligned with your values, look to see if there are alternatives and research their policies and practices.

**Part 3: What Choices for Action Do You Have?**

For the businesses that you feel are NOT aligned with your values or the issues you feel are important, let's consider your options.

1. Do you really need that product or service?
2. What would it mean for you to shift to a different business (for example, if you changed to a different grocery store, it might mean less convenience, higher prices, different products)?

**Part 4: Action—What Choice Makes Sense?**

1. Decide on, and shift to, a different business and send a letter explaining why you are taking your business elsewhere.
2. Stay with the business (for example, if you feel it is your only choice) and write a letter asking them to change their policies.
3. Look to see how you might get involved.

| Type of Business | Positive policies and practices | Negative policies and practices | Are there better alternatives? | What would it mean for you to shift? | What action could you take? |
|---|---|---|---|---|---|
| Bank or Credit Union: | | | | | |
| Grocery Store: | | | | | |
| Restaurants: | | | | | |
| Clothing: | | | | | |
| Investments (see below): | | | | | |
| Online Shopping: | | | | | |
| Other: | | | | | |
| | | | | | |

We can also take action by financially investing in and donating to organizations that show a commitment to the issues that we care about.

# Your Economic Power: Giving and Investing

If and when you have financial resources, giving can be an important way to help others. Whether we grew up learning lessons about sharing what we have with those who have less than us, or a principle that a certain amount of our income should be devoted to charitable causes, giving may be an integral part of what we see as our responsibility or our way of contributing.

## Giving

There is a distinction between charitable giving that benefits individuals and giving that fosters systemic change. Giving that focuses on providing for individuals in need is useful and can help organizations carry out services, provide resources, and support political and social campaigns. Yet, there are some important questions to raise in terms of how giving does, or does not, change the underlying system that keeps the inequities in place. In a 2011 *Smiley & West* talk show, Dr. Cornel West made this distinction:

> Philanthropy is a beautiful thing, that kind of charity is a marvelous thing, but never to be confused with justice. Never to be confused with the unfairness shot through the system and how the system operates, so you can be a Rockefeller, you can be a Bloomberg, you can be a Carnegie or whatever, you can be an Oprah Winfrey, and give money, that's a beautiful thing, it's individual and it does become a force of good in the lives of the person it affects. But that is qualitatively different than justice.

One of the criticisms of charitable donations is that it maintains the status quo. In other words, the person with financial and economic advantage maintains that advantage and chooses how and where their money is spent, while those who are disadvantaged generally remain disadvantaged, albeit with temporary relief due to the charity. *Poor* magazine, "a poor people led/Indigenous people led non-profit, grassroots, arts organization" in the San Francisco Bay Area (http://www.poormagazine.org/About%20Us), describes multiple critiques of philanthropy. Their "Revolutionary Giving" web page describes one issue and their solution in the following way.

> Philanthropy which has its roots in the Slave/Master "plantation" model, operates from the premise that people with money and/ or resources inherently hold more knowledge about money than people without money. Contrary, we believe that people who have struggled to survive, feed and clothe multiple family members and themselves in fact hold a deep scholarship about the use and distribution of resources. (http://www.poormagazine.org/rev_donor)

Karen Washington, a food justice activist and cofounder of Black Urban Growers, talks about the short-sightedness of "charitable" approaches to the lack of healthy food in economically poor neighborhoods, (https:// www.theguardian.com/society/2018/may/15/food-apartheid-food-deserts-racism-inequality-america-karen-washington-interview). She argues that the term *food desert* is problematic because it ignores the vibrancy and potential in neighborhoods that have traditionally limited access to food and that it ignores the systems of racial and economic oppression that created and maintains that inequity. She suggests that *food apartheid* is a better term because it acknowledges the long-standing influence of racism in food and opportunity. She also criticizes the pattern of outsiders to the neighborhood coming in with their own solutions, organizations, or businesses trying to address a problem. She suggests an alternative approach.

> I wake up dreaming that my neighborhood has been given capital, has been given opportunity, has been given finance, that we can own our stores and businesses. Why is it that outsiders always have to come into our neighborhood to open a business? Why don't people with capital come into my neighborhood and think about investing in the people who already live here? Give them the capital, give them the means of financial literacy, teach them how to invest, teach them how to own homes, teach them how to own businesses. Give them that chance, instead of coming in and changing the dynamics and the complexion of our neighborhood.

As noted by Dr. Cornel West in the earlier quote, inequity and injustice are a result of systemic problems and a legacy of oppression rather than simply a lack of resources. Just as economic inequity is a result of structural oppression, the privilege of wealth and financial stability comes as a result of historical oppression. Financial support is needed to help meet immediate survival needs of those impacted by that legacy of oppression, yet a framework that also includes support for structural change and investment that recognizes the rights and wisdom of people receiving the funds is closer to what *Poor* magazine calls "Revolutionary Giving."

The history in the United States—and all over the world—of the theft of Indigenous land through settlers, colonizers, and war has resulted in tremendous economic and social inequity. The Sogorea Te Land Trust is one example of an effort to reshape what it means to give financially (http://sogoreate-landtrust.com/shuumi-land-tax/). This urban Indigenous women-led community organization in the San Francisco Bay Area "facilitates the return of Chochenyo and Karkin Ohlone lands in the San Francisco Bay Area to Indigenous stewardship." They have developed a "Shuumi Land Tax," reflected in a map that shows the Indigenous communities that have resided for thousands of years on the land that the donor now lives on. The Shuumi Land Tax system is their way of providing an opportunity for settlers to begin to pay to live on the Indigenous land. They describe the historical impact and its relation to giving this way:

> If you live on Chochenyo and Karkin Ohlone land, you are inadvertently benefitting from the genocide waged against the Ohlone people and the theft of their land. Whether you know it or not,

however you feel about it, this is an inescapable fact. The civic infrastructure, the economic system, the private development and the consumption of natural resources in our society are all connected to and in different ways built upon the colonial occupation of this land and the violent displacement of the Ohlone. Paying the Shuumi Land Tax is a small way to acknowledge this legacy and contribute to its healing.

Although paying the land tax is voluntary, the Sogorea Te Land Trust provides a formula to determine an appropriate amount of the giver's land tax, including the specific location of residence, rented or owned, and the size of dwelling reflecting the amount of resources consumed. So, for example, if you own a four-bedroom house, your land tax would be higher than if you rent a one-bedroom apartment.

There are some questions we can ask when we consider donating as social action to increase the likelihood that we are supporting change. How much of the donation will go to the people or cause that we care about? (Hint: Resources such as Charity Navigator can be helpful to understand how the money is spent.) If the organization or cause is focused on people, how are the people most affected involved in positions of leadership to determine how the money is spent and how the organization runs? To what extent are the organization's efforts sustainable over time and aimed at changing inequity and injustice systematically? Giving as everyday social action can be a useful way to contribute funds for social change work being done by organizations.

## Investing

It has become less and less common for Americans to have enough money to invest. Although retirement accounts have become more of a luxury given shifts in employment policies and opportunities, for those who do have investments, socially responsible investing is an important way to consider how your money is supporting justice, access, and equity—or alternatively, how it perpetuates injustice. Understanding this could require looking at a company's practices regarding production of their goods, their distribution practices, the environmental impact of the product, their labor policies, their international policies, the products they make, and other aspects of their business. Often, retirement and other investment funds are made up of portfolios of many different businesses. Over the past couple of decades, there have been more opportunities for funds that are chosen around particular values; for example, excluding any businesses that produce or sell firearms, tobacco, alcohol, petroleum, or other products or that have particular labor or environmental policies.

Fortunately, there are a lot of resources to help you sort through this. Amy Livingston, in a Money Crashers article (https://www.moneycrashers.com/socially-responsible-investing/), provides great tips for beginning to think about socially responsible investing. Further, the Forum for Sustainable and Responsible Investment (https://www.ussif.org/about), a nonprofit organization, provides regular reports and information regarding details that may be important to consider when looking at companies and investment portfolios.

Another option to consider is local investing, where your funds are directly invested in locally owned businesses. Michael Shuman, writing for SOCAP (Social Capital Markets), describes a number of strategies for small investors to shift the way they think about their money and their community to consider the benefits of grassroots investing (https://socialcapitalmarkets.net/2015/06/invest-locally-10-tools-for-grassroots-investing/). Considering how you use your money, whether it's what you buy or where you invest, is an important avenue for social action as a regular part of your life.

## Social Media and Effective Action

Social media has been brought up throughout this workbook in terms of long-term strategies and now again in everyday action, as it has infiltrated much of our lives and how we know the world. Social media has become a central force in sharing information, opinions, and news. In fact, in an August 2017 survey, 67% of U.S. adults said they receive at least some of their news through social media sources (http://www.journalism.org/2017/09/07/news-use-across-social-media-platforms-2017/). An October 2016 survey, the Political Environment on Social Media, looked at people's connection to social media, what they thought about politics in social media, and how connected social media was to whether people actually took action on political or social change issues (http://www.pewinternet.org/2016/10/25/political-engagement-and-social-media/). The study found that people who were politically engaged (e.g., reported that they voted regularly in elections, volunteered or donated to political parties or organizations) felt that social media could "bring new voices into the political discussion" and "help people get involved with issues that matter to them."

Alicia Garza, cofounder of Black Lives Matter, noted that engagement in social media doesn't necessarily translate into effective action. She explained, "What it takes to get people from liking and sharing and retweeting to organising is a hard and long process" (https://www.theguardian.

com/us-news/2016/sep/02/alicia-garza-on-the-beauty-and-the-burden-of-black-lives-matter). "Slacktivism," or "the practice of supporting a political or social cause by means such as social media or online petitions, characterized as involving very little effort or commitment" (https://en.oxforddictionaries.com/definition/slacktivism), has been criticized as a way for people to feel good about doing something without actually doing very much. In an introduction to an excellent Jody Williams blog about getting involved, Outspeak writes:

> We're constantly consuming memes, viral videos, selfies, on-demand TV, and mobile games, all of which are meant to keep us "connected" longer. They encourage our desire to lounge around for hours of inaction for just one more scroll, one more snap, one more episode of Kevin Spacey in his *House of Cards*. We may be aware of societal issues through our digital feeds, but as a result activism is often replaced by slacktivism. (https://www.huffingtonpost.com/entry/jody-williams-on-activism_b_10010538.html)

In fact, some research by Kirk Kristofferson, Katherine White, and John Peloza in 2014 found that people who "like" a cause on Facebook or similar social media sites are no more likely to take action or support that cause in any other way in their life. So, how can social media be helpful as a tool or strategy for taking action? Professor Nicholas Mirzoeff from New York University describes the interaction between a successful "visual activism" approach, such as Black Lives Matter, and social media. He argues that

> What's so crucial about making visual activism work is that it catalyses real life social activism through social media. If it's just on social media, then very little will follow from that. But if, by seeing things, people are impelled to take action themselves, and they are helped to find out how to take that action themselves, then change can result. (http://www.abc.net.au/news/2017-10-25/activism-is-broken-heres-how-we-fix-it/9077372)

There are some great examples of how the Internet and social media have been important tools in activism and working toward change. Odağ, Uluğ, and Solak (2016) showed how online collective actions, using social media, were critical to the Gezi Park protests in Turkey. A news report by the British Broadcasting Corporation described how photos and videos of violence toward protesters that were posted on Flickr, Tumblr and YouTube helped the world to be more aware of the situation in Turkey. Further, Twitter and Facebook posts helped to share information that was vital for protesters for engaging in, and surviving, protests and government retaliation (https://www.bbc.com/news/world-europe-22772352).

Another social media strategy was described in the Advocates for Youth Activists Toolkit:

> In the spring of 2012, Advocates for Youth along with other organizations decided to put pressure on Congress to support birth control coverage under the Affordable Care Act. We utilized a social media strategy asking youth activists to take pictures with valentines' reading "Congress, listen up or we're breaking up, birth control matters." These valentines were tweeted at members of Congress with the hashtag #bc4us. Over 1,600 people took pictures and tweeted them at Congress, to demonstrate young people's support for no cost birth control. The collection of valentines was later compiled in a book and presented to House Minority Leader Nancy Pelosi, to further extend the campaign and bring even more attention to the issue. This form of social media pressure on members of Congress helped to show them that their constituents were watching and wanted them to take action to ensure birth control coverage under the Affordable Care Act. (http://www.advocatesforyouth.org/publications/publications-a-z/2229-youth-activists-toolkit#creatingastrategy)

The toolkit emphasizes that social media and online actions must be connected and extend beyond the Internet. For example, petition signatures can be delivered in person to the decision maker or legislator and with a photo op that is then posted online to publicize that the decision maker received the message. The Toolbox also suggests that the use of social media is an important way to make activism inclusive, providing different venues for people to participate who may not be able to physically attend actions.

Social media has brought awareness of a multitude of issues and events that people may have never heard of and resulted in donations as well as people getting involved as volunteers, attending events, contacting legislators through emails and phone calls, and getting motivated to actually vote in elections. Social media, through pictures, videos, and human stories, can help people feel connected in a more personal way. This lays the groundwork for action but does not guarantee it and runs the risk of enticing the user to stay in the virtual world believing they are doing something. At this point, I (Rebecca) have to confess: in the past couple of years, I engaged a lot in retweeting stories and articles about social justice in employment and education. It was tempting when upsetting events and reports come hourly, to check Twitter whenever I had a free moment and retweet because it seemed that so many unjust things were happening about education and employment. Although I felt well informed about real opportunities for actions, such as rallies to protect Indigenous land from development, this pattern also began to feel like a distraction from actually doing things, like writing letters to legislators. This past year, I chose to limit the amount of time I spend on social media, in part because it felt overwhelming, my day job became very consuming, and I wanted to focus on writing this book. However, I find that I have become less informed, less able to address sociopolitical events that affect my students and community, and I am more likely to miss announcements about political and community events and actions. I am now trying to find balance and strategies for using the informative aspects of social media and tie it more closely to regular action. One example is the way I can use social media to inform and enhance my participation in solidarity with our Indigenous community members and trying to raise awareness in the local community about the sacredness of local land and its destruction through development. I can learn about city council meetings, letter writing campaigns and ceremonies as well as how to participate respectfully in these events as a White woman so that when I show up, I am more likely to show up in solidarity as opposed to as a voyeur or "savior."

Social media is a tool, yet virtual action alone is not the same as real action. Adapting Gandhi's famous quote, Daisy Prado emphasizes, "Be the change you want to see in the world, don't just tweet the change you want to see in the world." In all likelihood, the best approach is multiple approaches. Social media, direct action, visible action, gradual and subtle action, community coalitions, as well as directly contacting legislators and decision makers are all approaches that may be useful yet have different benefits and costs. Timing, resources, and people who are involved can influence what strategy you use. Unforeseeable opportunities or obstacles sometimes nudge your movement one way or the other.

There are many different approaches to consider when planning your strategies. In this next section, we broaden our perspective again toward the big picture with an eye to how we can evaluate which options or strategies might suit a particular situation or issue.

## Evaluating and Deciding Which Strategies Are Best for the Situation

As you can see in the Strategies described above, there are many possible avenues for action. Regardless of whether you already know what action you will take (or are taking), this section is designed to help you think through aspects of the alternatives and be better prepared. There are often multiple avenues to accomplish similar goals, yet there are different benefits and costs for each avenue.

## Evaluating Benefits

Of course, the most obvious benefit, in the best of all worlds, is that change happens, and injustice is rectified. This is often easier to see with immediate or close-range issues. Progress is more difficult to see when dealing with large-scale or systemic barriers, oppression, and injustice. There are a few aspects to consider when reflecting on the potential benefits of any action:

- Does the action contribute to accomplishing the goal or sub-goal?

- Will the action lay the next steps in a way that will benefit the people affected and the people working on the action?

- Who benefits from the change or action?

- Are the people who are most affected by the problem engaged in the solution (either directly or by consultation)?

- Is the problem less likely to occur again as a result of the action?

- Will more people care about this issue and join as allies?

"Bay Area Stands United Against Hate Week" featured activities in communities all around the San Francisco Bay Area organized by community alliances in a loosely coordinated effort to call for unity and stand against actions of discrimination. One community alliance (students, community members, school and county representatives) chose as one of their events a unity poetry/art slam with the following goals: build compassion for marginalized group members, raise awareness about the positive aspects of inclusion and the impact of exclusion and hate speech, and increase involvement. Student members took leadership and coordinated poetry performances and an art exhibit of paintings and sculptures reflecting themes of unity and pain felt as a result of exclusion. If we evaluate the strategy using the above questions as a guide, the event had the following characteristics: multiple stakeholders were involved, publicity and the event included widespread messaging, and many voices were heard through art and poetry. In short, some benefits of this event included emotional and educational enrichment, representation, engagement, community coming together, advocacy for issues, cultural and individual pride, and inclusion.

The final note is that the outcomes of action or a strategy may not always be known to you. It can be challenging knowing whether what you have done, or what you helped to do, is the best option. Checking in with trusted others and people who are working toward the same goals and/or are affected by the issues or problems you are trying to address can be one way to get a sense of whether you are going in the right direction. The main point is to stop, reflect, and gather information before proceeding.

## Assessing the Costs: Thinking About Consequences and Repercussions

As with benefits, we can sometimes predict the costs and see them clearly. Sometimes we can't. Costs are directly related to the power and privilege we have in a situation and in our lives overall; generally, power and privilege can act as buffers to minimize costs or can exacerbate the consequences. Costs can take many forms such as resources (financial, job, money, time), social (loss or strain of relationships), emotional (isolation, fear, harassment, stress, discomfort), freedom, and physical (safety, physical harm). Some costs are simply the resources required to carry out an action. Other costs are consequences or repercussions that come as backlash against us given actions we've taken. It's helpful to look ahead and consider whether the costs of a particular strategy or avenue for action are reasonable and manageable (e.g., the action is worth the cost), or unmanageable and too costly.

There are many considerations when evaluating the possible costs. Some of these costs may affect us personally—our responsibilities, imbalance in our work and life, our emotional and physical health, and others. Some consequences are professional; for example, risk of job loss, shunning in our employment setting, extra work assigned, and others. Some consequences cross over both (e.g., legal or financial costs). Timing, power, and the larger context all influence consequences.

The timing of events may affect the consequences. The consequences may feel too great at one time and may feel acceptable at another, depending on other aspects of our lives or our well-being, as well as our positions of power or lack thereof. For example, if you have young children, time away from family often has higher costs than when children are older and more independent. Similarly, time away from family has high costs as parents get older. In another example, our power relative to others may change over time. If you are new in a job, you likely have less influence to make changes, and the consequences may be more severe than if you are established in the job.

Understanding power involves knowing how much we have or don't have in a situation and how much power others have to impose consequences on us if they don't like our message or action. Power takes many forms, such as the ability to force someone to do something, to give or take away resources or freedom, to allow access, to influence opinion, and others. When you are allied with large numbers of people who are all working toward the same goal, you have more power. Obviously, people in decision-making positions who have access to resources or who can withhold resources have power. Within the United States there is a historical context in which people who have money and ownership have had economic and political power and reflected largely White, male, heterosexual, Christian perspectives. Thus, they have had more power to support initiatives that are aligned with their perspectives. Raji Hunjan and Jethro Pettit have a great guide to understand and strategize power in taking action: *Power: A Practical Guide for Facilitating Social Change* (http://www.participatorymethods. org/sites/participatorymethods.org/files/Power-A-Practical-Guide-for-Facilitating-Social-Change_0.pdf). This and other resources can be helpful in understanding and recognizing the influences of power on the work we consider doing.

Other considerations relate to very real differences in how we are treated based on our identities and the risks we face, depending on whether we are targeted in the situation. We have mentioned numerous times the ways that we are each perceived in groups and how that shapes our choices and consequences. For example, if I (Rebecca) speak up about racism at a community meeting where the crowd is mostly White, I am less likely to be threatened or accused of having a personal grudge against White people. Although there might be a risk that some people won't like what I have to say and might think I'm too opinionated or "just trying to be politically correct," the consequences are less threatening. Alternatively, if I (Muninder) speak up in that same meeting, I am more likely to be dismissed, accused of having a personal agenda or grudge, and may be threatened or experience other negative consequences.

There are also different emotional costs for each of us. For example, I (Rebecca) have not spent my life having to deal with culturally insensitive or racist behavior directed at me or my family. Until I began to understand racism more deeply in my early 20s, I most likely did not recognize many of these kinds of situations and thus did not pay an emotional cost each time they came up—whereas I (Muninder) have experienced discriminatory and racist behavior all of my life. It is exhausting, and when it comes up, even having to decide each time whether to speak up adds an additional emotional stressor. Each of us has to consider how harmful the consequences will be and decide what to do.

An important question when reflecting and evaluating various strategies focuses on recognizing when the risky feeling is an important signal of a real threat and when it is mostly our own fear acting up. Similarly, once we accurately identify the risk (to the best of our ability with the information available), we can hopefully make a decision about whether the action is worth the risk or how to engage in the action with an acceptable amount of risk. For example, if I (Rebecca) notice inequity in my workplace and speak out against it, my goal is to remedy an injustice. In situations where my job is not secure and I depend on that job for my family or my own well-being, I may feel that the risk of job loss is too great. Even though not speaking out may feel costly in terms of the emotional cost, the financial cost may be too great. For another person, that same cost of a job may be acceptable if they feel like they have other job options or other financial resources. Further, not speaking out may be costly to our well-being, our relationships, and our sense of integrity and fairness, so we speak out and deal with the consequences. Only you can know whether the benefits outweigh the costs for you, your life, and your family.

As you consider the issue you have chosen to focus on and think about the possibilities for strategies to address that issue, reflect on the benefits and costs of each approach. In the previous sections on strategies, we have noted a few possible consequences or considerations regarding that strategy. This has not been an exhaustive discussion though, as the costs depend to some extent on the circumstances. Having said this, it is important to investigate policies, rules, laws, and practices when weighing the costs for the strategies you consider. This way, you can make an informed choice about how to proceed given what you know about the possible consequences. For example, if you are choosing to do a public display of resistance through art, maybe an impromptu performance in a public space, look into that community's history of such demonstrations and how they were received by the community, businesses, security, and law enforcement. Are there permit requirements? Are there some spaces where this is allowed and other spaces where it is not allowed? This information will be helpful to you when deciding what kinds of risks you are willing to take and whether the benefits outweigh the costs. Do you want to pursue the permit process, or does that interfere in taking action? If the process is prohibitive, are the potential consequences and costs manageable if you work outside the system? Additionally, the following exercise can help you to think about possible steps or approaches to your strategy that will help minimize the costs and maximize benefits. Gathering wisdom gained by groups who have taken similar action in the past can provide you with important information about things you might want to consider.

ACTIVITY 6.18

## Your Analysis: One of Your Issues

### Part 1: Examining the Issue

1. What do you want to see happen? What is the goal?
2. What levels are possible for action?
   a. Individual interactions:
   b. Community or organizational:
   c. Societal, federal, or state legislative levels:
3. Pick four possible actions and approaches and describe them below:
   a. Option 1:
   b. Option 2:
   c. Option 3:
   d. Option 4:

### Part 2: Benefit and Cost Analysis

For this next part, consider the benefits and costs of each of the different options you identified.

1. **Benefits and costs for the goal or community.** How might this further the goals or alleviate the issue? Are there costs or setbacks that may arise because of the action?

|  | Option 1 | Option 2 | Option 3 | Option 4 |
|---|---|---|---|---|
| Benefits: |  |  |  |  |
| Costs: |  |  |  |  |

2. **Benefits and costs to you personally.** Might there be an impact, positively or negatively, in your personal life?

|  | Option 1 | Option 2 | Option 3 | Option 4 |
|---|---|---|---|---|
| Benefits: |  |  |  |  |
| Costs: |  |  |  |  |

3. **Benefits and costs for your job or profession.** Might there be an impact, positively or negatively?

| | Option 1: | Option 2: | Option 3: | Option 4: |
|---|---|---|---|---|
| Benefits: | | | | |
| Costs: | | | | |

Now that you have examined the costs and benefits of a variety of strategies, consider the following questions:

- Which strategies seem to benefit the community and have the most potential to achieve the desired outcome?
- Of these strategies, which are least costly or have manageable costs?
- What would you do next to create, initiate, or collaborate on this strategy?

The considerations for strategies and possible benefits and consequences is an exercise that you may want to circle back to periodically. Sometimes the outcomes are not clear until we actually engage in the activity. New information or opportunities may come to light later on. For now, given the work you have just done, think about how to communicate this to others. Revisiting your elevator speech can get you started.

## ACTIVITY 6.19

## Finishing Your Elevator Speech

We come to the time for you to finish your elevator speech! You have identified your issue, located yourself in relation to the issue, brought together compelling information about the issue, and now you can identify what you are doing to address it as well as what you want from the person who will listen to your elevator speech.

Go to the last draft of your speech from the point where you added information about your issue (Activity 6.3).

1. Introduce yourself, your position and place.
2. Share your issue and why it is important.

3. What are you doing? (One or two sentences; for example, "I am sharing information with community members to help support organizations that are providing legal assistance to the families to protect their children and apply for asylum.)

4. What do you want from the listener? (One sentence; for example, if you have decided on particular strategies, "It is urgent that we let our state and federal representatives know that these families deserve a chance to apply for asylum and be reunited with their children.")

Strategies are often the core of what we picture when we think of getting engaged and working toward social justice. Yet, one of the biggest challenges we often face is how to sustain our energy, commitment, and ourselves as we fight for justice. Sustainability, the fourth *S*, is a critical area of reflection and one that we often take for granted.

# chapter seven

# Sustainability

## Healthy Mind, Heart, Body, and Spirit

Sustainability

*Caring for myself is not self-indulgence, it is self-preservation, and that is an act of political warfare.*

—Audre Lorde

Sustainability is essential to keep moving toward positive change, surviving, and even thriving in the face of challenges. Being engaged in action about issues we care about can be good for our health, yet can also challenge our health, responsibilities, and relationships. For us to have an impact on issues we care about, WE are one of the most important tools. Personal sustainability means that part of social action means that you, your well-being, and your life matter. Part of the work that needs to be done includes balancing social action with planfulness that help us to live our lives, keep us healthy, and honor the priorities we have, such as family, community, and spirituality. Sustainability is critical for effective social action, not just so we can be more effective in our work but also because the harmful effects of not taking care of ourselves often result in us quitting the fight altogether, taking our potential and our contributions with us. Even worse, we may actually become harmful to others and the causes we care about when we are not doing well.

Based on their conversations with peace activists who had experienced burnout and were able to persist in their activism, Downton and Wehr (1998) drew a full picture of the elements that seemed important. First, they found that life patterns (family, money, career flexibility, and social networks) as well as engagement with others who were committed to the issues (family, social movement, and church) created the availability and motivation to get involved in the first place. Then, the things that helped activists stay involved despite challenges included feelings of bonding with others in the movement, sharing the vision of a positive outcome, ability to manage support and criticism, feeling rewards for their activism, managing burnout, integrating their activism with their life, and navigating competing responsibilities. This research highlights a couple of key points that we mentioned earlier and are worth discussing again. First, each of us knows our own life demands and can reflect on what kind and how much activism is feasible for our health and that of our loved ones. There are times when we may be more involved and other times we may be less involved. The purpose of sustainability is to emphasize that it is an integral part of addressing issues we care about. Social justice change is a long process, like a marathon; it is important to pace yourself, ensure you hydrate and are well nourished, have support and encouragement, and recognize when you are injured. Just like time is needed to reflect on our strengths, build solidarity, and act on strategies, there is also time needed for sustainability.

In this chapter, we will talk about the challenges of sustaining ourselves and our work, what sustainability might look like, and strategies for continuing to move forward in social action while maintaining or recovering from challenges to our well-being. In the second half of the chapter, we provide activities to help you think about and make space for your life in the midst of your social action.

## Challenges of Sustaining Ourselves

There are many challenges commonly experienced by people engaged in social action and activism. If you feel stressed or challenged, you are not alone! It can be helpful to understand what researchers have found about wellness related to social action and activism and look at how this might apply to your life and work. First, let's consider the following activity to get a sense of how you are doing in various aspects of your well-being. We will reflect back on this activity throughout this chapter to look at challenges to our well-being and then to move toward health and wellness.

## How Am I Doing?

In this activity, reflect on beliefs and behaviors that you hold. Be honest with yourself. This is your opportunity to look at the path you're on and make adjustments that could help you stay healthy. You will be able to use these results later when we focus on your health and wellness.

In the following questions, reflect on the past three months or so and mark an **X** in the box relating to how often this describes you. The tables below consider six different areas that affect our wellness: emotional (E), physical (P), mental (M), social (S), spiritual (Sp), and contextual (C).

1. **How am I doing emotionally?**

|  | Never | Rarely | Sometimes | Often | Always |
|---|---|---|---|---|---|
| I feel guilty when I don't stand up for what I know is right. (E) |  |  |  |  |  |
| I feel sad or anxious, sometimes without a clear reason. (E) |  |  |  |  |  |
| It seems like no matter what we do, we can't stop the injustice; it feels hopeless. (E) |  |  |  |  |  |
| I get frustrated because I don't get recognized for the work I do. (E) |  |  |  |  |  |
| I feel like so many people suffer so much that it's not right for me to feel sad, tired, or like I want a break. (E) |  |  |  |  |  |

As you reflect on your responses above, if you notice a lot of *Often* or *Always* answers, you may want to pay special attention to the emotional health discussion later in this chapter.

2. **How am I doing physically?**

| | Never | Rarely | Sometimes | Often | Always |
|---|---|---|---|---|---|
| I feel physically exhausted. (P) | | | | | |
| I'm so busy that I don't get much exercise or take care of myself very well. (P) | | | | | |
| I have trouble sleeping because I am distressed or thinking about what I should do. (P) | | | | | |
| I overeat, drink too much alcohol, or use other drugs to deal with the stress. (P) | | | | | |
| I have physical pains (e.g., headaches, stomachaches) or get sick a lot. (P) | | | | | |

As you reflect on your responses above, if you notice a lot of *Often* or *Always* answers, attending to your physical health may be helpful. These physical stressors may reflect general health issues or may be exacerbated by stress.

3. **How am I doing mentally?**

| | Never | Rarely | Sometimes | Often | Always |
|---|---|---|---|---|---|
| I feel overwhelmed thinking about all the ways I should be involved. (M) | | | | | |
| It seems like if I don't step up, no one else will. (M) | | | | | |
| I end up taking on more than I can really handle. (M) | | | | | |
| I shouldn't burden other people with my worries. (M) | | | | | |
| I am distracted thinking about injustice and what I should be doing. (M) | | | | | |

As you reflect on your responses above, if you notice a lot of *Often* or *Always* answers, attending to your wellness in terms of your thinking process and mental energy may be helpful. Sometimes, we get caught up in thought patterns that are stressful or don't allow ourselves a mental rest, at times not being compassionate with ourselves.

4. **How am I doing socially or in my relationships?**

| | Never | Rarely | Sometimes | Often | Always |
|---|---|---|---|---|---|
| It seems like there are few people who care about the issues that I care about. (S) | | | | | |
| Other activists in my group expect too much from me. (S) | | | | | |
| I have trouble saying no when I'm working with a group. (S) | | | | | |
| I am torn between spending time with family, friends, and engaging in activism. (S) | | | | | |
| When I am around other activists, I feel disconnected or disrespected. (S) | | | | | |

As you reflect on your responses above, if you notice a lot of *Often* or *Always* answers, attending to your wellness in terms of social engagements and relationships may be helpful. Are you feeling stress or tension in your social connections and relationships related to your time or effort to address injustice? In addition, considering some of the discussion in the Solidarity chapter may provide some insights.

5. **How am I doing spiritually?**

| | Never | Rarely | Sometimes | Often | Always |
|---|---|---|---|---|---|
| It seems like none of it really means anything in the long run. (Sp) | | | | | |
| I feel like my beliefs about spirituality (or religion) are not helpful to me. (Sp) | | | | | |
| I feel like I'm missing something spiritually. (Sp) | | | | | |
| I feel lost and disconnected spiritually. (Sp) | | | | | |
| I feel conflicts between my religious or spiritual beliefs and the issues that come up in my social action. (Sp) | | | | | |

As you reflect on your responses above, if you notice a lot of *Often* or *Always* answers, attending to your wellness in terms of your spiritual life may be helpful. Everyone has their own set of beliefs, whether it is belief in a higher power or belief that there is no higher power. This category refers more to how you <u>feel</u> about the beliefs you hold rather than the beliefs themselves.

6. **What is the context I live in?**

| | Never | Rarely | Sometimes | Often | Always |
|---|---|---|---|---|---|
| In my community or neighborhood, it seems like there are very few people who share important aspects of my identity (ethnicity, sexual orientation, religion, etc.). (C) | | | | | |
| There is legislation (or practices) that prevents people from my racial group, sexual orientation, gender, ability status, religion, or other identity from having the same rights as other people. (C) | | | | | |
| If I speak out against injustice, I often get called too "sensitive." (C) | | | | | |
| There are higher rates of violence toward people like me than other groups (e.g., gender, sexual orientation, race, religion, etc.). (C) | | | | | |
| There are documented hate crimes and/or discrimination against my communities/ identities. (C) | | | | | |

As you reflect on your responses above, if you notice a lot of *Often* or *Always* answers, it may be helpful to acknowledge the impact of your context in which you live on your health and wellness. You may encounter systemic hostility in your environment or in society regarding your identity and that may be affecting your well-being in significant ways. Challenges that you experience due to the context you live in may, in fact, be an area where you are doing social change work. Or it may not be. Regardless, as we discussed earlier in this workbook, sometimes just holding an identity that is targeted means that we may end up having to deal with situations and hostility without choosing that. We end up having to choose whether to react, how to stay safe, and what the consequences might be for anything we do, even as basic as "Did they really just say that?"

As you think about the six different areas above, some questions may resonate with you, and others might not. This is certainly not an exhaustive list, and you may have a better sense of how you are doing than what you see here. It is normal to feel some of these some of the time. The problem comes when it is too much, too often, or interferes with your life, relationships, social action, or self-compassion. This activity is meant to stimulate your thinking about your wellness in each of these activities and to consider stress or tension you may be feeling in particular areas that might benefit from more healthful approaches in your life. It is intended to provide an alert for you to an area (or areas) that may be helpful to pay attention to. It is not necessarily a definitive statement about your life. An important part of sustainability is taking a look at how we can build up our resilience and support systems in all aspects of our lives, including those in the above activity, so we are better able to sustain ourselves and our ability to contribute to meaningful social action.

The monumental social changes that we have seen over the past decades could not have been possible without enormous effort on the part of many people working for many years. We often see the outcomes but not the costs, psychological and physical, that can be felt as a result of such big efforts. Despite the positive effects of collective action, activism, and other social change efforts, we may also experience exhaustion, anxiety, withdrawal, broken relationships, and burnout, among others. In the next few paragraphs, we dive into exploring what is known about burnout and risks, and then turn to explore the healthy ways we can work to maximize the benefits of our social action and minimize the wear and tear.

## Burnout

Research on activism burnout has helped us understand the toll that social action can take, as well as how to prevent and recover from burnout. The term *burnout* is often used causally in everyday conversation to express a range of negative feelings. However, "burnout" actually means something very specific and is different from simple exhaustion, boredom, depression, and other emotions. The term burnout was coined in the early 1970s by Herbert Freudenberger (Freudenberger & Richelson, 1980) and was defined as a reaction to high levels of persistent occupational stress. This phenomenon was later studied extensively by Christina Maslach and a number of her colleagues, focusing on all types of occupations and work that involve emotional stressors. Burnout specifically refers to a cluster of symptoms resulting from chronic and long-term stress related to one's work. It is different from having a bad day or stress from a particular instance. Rather, an essential aspect of burnout is that the stressor is relatively unrelenting over time and has no clear resolution. We may feel the effects of burnout emotionally (e.g., numbness, sadness, anxiety, despair), mentally (e.g., mental exhaustion, thoughts of worthlessness, feelings of helplessness), physically (e.g., physical exhaustion, chronic illness), behaviorally (e.g., self-defeating behaviors, substance abuse), and motivationally (e.g., apathy, disillusionment). These effects often appear gradually, so we don't recognize that it is happening until we are already suffering and are unable to easily fix the problem. In fact, one of the most difficult challenges of burnout is that we become exhausted, we believe that we can do little about it, and sometimes we believe that it is our fault. Because of this, it is often hard for us to shift to a more positive place. For example, if you experience burnout in your job, the symptoms of burnout may make it hard for you to be energetic and confident searching for a new job. Burnout in activism can have a similar pattern. Ongoing stress related to the systems we are challenging, our limited ability to impact immediate change, hostility by those we oppose, and even tension within the group we are working can result in similar symptoms, making it difficult for us to continue as effective change agents.

There are a number of other issues that come up in activism, given assumptions and beliefs that sometimes go along with social justice work. For example, we may feel that we should be working tirelessly because the communities we are fighting for have faced so much; the privilege of taking a break feels selfish. In addition, we may feel a constant sense of urgency and hypervigilance (always having to pay attention) because so many incidents of injustice arise frequently as do opportunities to take action. It can start to feel overwhelming and dizzying to keep up with all of the everyday social actions, not to mention the big collective actions.

Another important variation has to do with our positionality in relation to oppression and the issues we care about. As a conscious Person of Color in a racist society, there may be daily challenges to one's integrity, sense of belonging, and worth. "Persistence is our resistance" is a mantra to recognize that sometimes the act of persisting, whether in education or our community, is an act of resistance itself and the most important thing to do, especially for people who face marginalization. For others of us, we have identities that are not targeted regularly with oppressive acts; thus, we are not subjected daily to personal affronts, and we have more choices about when to fight. Still, we may feel assaulted by the harm that is done to those we love and the issues we care about. We may also feel a sense of guilt and a responsibility to work toward justice unceasingly because we are not subjected to injustice in the same way others might be. In both cases, the risk of burnout, exhaustion, and fatigue can interfere with us being able to effectively act.

Activist Trauma Support, an organization dedicated to helping activists recognize and recover from burnout, argues that often we believe that burnout is just part of the process and the toll to be paid, but it doesn't need to be that way. In a more helpful way, they suggest that we can use symptoms of burnout as warning signs, alerting us to the need to step back and reflect on how we are working, how we are relating to others, and how we are caring (or not caring) for ourselves (https://www.activist-trauma.net).

## Focusing on Our Health and Wellness

Despite the challenges of participating in social action, there is also plenty of evidence that being engaged and active around issues we care about can be good for us. Tod Sloan, a friend and critical psychologist who blogged about systemic change and the relationship to his own health challenges, wrote:

> we tend to think that our work to make the world a better place and to make better, healthier, happier lives for ourselves are disconnected, and even go in different directions (as cases of activist burnout indicate, from overemphasizing the first in a disconnected way). But, clearly, the self-health-lifestyle changes one wants to make often rely on participating in the construction of solutions and better ways in communities, regions, nations, and globally.

Some research has shown that being involved in collective action can actually help reduce feelings of stress and other negative psychological effects felt by people who are in targeted groups. For example, in a 2014 study by Cirleen DeBlaere and her colleagues, sexual minority Women of Color (LGB) who were engaged in collective action seemed to experience lower psychological stress than those who were not. Dawn Szymanski and Gina Owens, in their 2009 study of Women of Color involved in feminist collective action, found that high levels of involvement seemed to buffer the negative effects of sexism.

**FIGURE 7.1** Four aspects of sustainability: Head, heart, body, and spirit

Still, working to eliminate injustice and toward social change can bring challenges to our health as evidenced by the research described above. This research and wisdom of activists also provides guidance about things that we can do to maintain our health and wellness, prevent burnout, and integrate healthful approaches into our social action strategies. In particular, research that has looked at how activists have been able to stay in the struggle despite challenges has uncovered a few gems that can be helpful in thinking about our own sustainability. We can think of healthful social action as representing the head (your mind and mental well-being), heart (your emotional health and your relationships), body (your physical well-being), and spirit (your sense of connection to something greater than yourself or the thing that anchors you to your beliefs and values).

As you reflect on your responses to the "How are you doing?" activity at the beginning of this chapter (Activity 7.1), consider the different areas where you may need a little extra attention. These realms are all connected, and although we talk about each area separately, the overlap and stress in one area affects other areas. Similarly, when we care for one area, we care for all.

# The Head: Our Mental Well-Being

Mental well-being can be about developing stronger skills and knowledge to help manage our social action endeavors as well as giving us a break from the mental energy required by engagement. There is ideally a balance between being mentally active and mentally at rest. We may find that engaging with other people who share our interests and concerns is inspiring and energizing mentally. Staying engaged with information and current events related to the issues we care about can be stimulating (especially when the news is good). Still, it is essential to also give yourself a break, an opportunity to reflect, or even an opportunity to let your mind get lost in something completely unrelated (e.g., watching an insect, a sunset, or a silly movie). Inspiration and mental stimulation can foster an engaged mind through laughter, nature, art, poetry, or whatever activates your mind in a healthy way.

**FIGURE 7.2** The head: Our mental well-being

When our minds are overly engaged, especially in stressful ways, we may develop mental fatigue, which can spread to physical fatigue or illness as well as thinking patterns that are not helpful. For example, our ability to maintain a clear and grounded perspective of events and distress around us relies on mental stability. Many of the issues we care about can trigger distress, and then we may have a harder time recognizing and dealing with forces or actions that oppose the work we are trying to do. Sometimes we end up feeling like everything is so urgent and important that we have to be working on it all the time and there is no time to decompress or step back and get perspective.

A number of studies have noted common themes around mental well-being and activist sustainability, providing recommendations for a healthy mind and mental coping. The study we mentioned earlier by Downton and Wehr (1998) found that activists who were able to learn how to manage criticism and negativity were better able to sustain their involvement. They described several strategies used to deal with critics, especially those with opposing beliefs: "they [the activists] discounted them knowing they were based on irreconcilable differences of belief; they insulated themselves by limiting their contact with the critics; and they employed humor to remove the sting from harsh words" (p. 543). We would add that it is helpful to distinguish between criticism that is malicious and disagreeable and criticism that may actually be helpful in reflecting on the approaches we have taken. When we feel healthy and stable, we are better able to hear criticism that could be helpful in assessing whether we are meeting our objectives in the best way possible.

Research by Kovan and Dirkx (2003) found that professional development helped reenergize activists. Similarly, other research has found that some activists found that viewing their activism as a form of personal growth was helpful. Paul Gorski (2015) looked at how mindfulness techniques can help activists address a number of challenges related to burnout. The activists he talked to described three ways they felt mindfulness was helpful. First, they shared that they were better able to find a balance between activism and self-care without blame or guilt. Second, they reported that mindfulness helped them slow down or step back to "see the big picture and letting go of the pressure to eliminate injustice instantaneously" (p. 706). And, third, they believed that it helped them manage stress and anxiety. Mindfulness practice, rooted in Buddhist philosophy, integrates breathing with attention to the present moment and release from judgment and preoccupation. There are many different forms and guides for using mindfulness, some of which are applied in everyday activities such as walking meditation, eating meditation, or sitting meditation. Interestingly, the activists that Gorski interviewed also described several ways that their mindfulness practice improved the effectiveness of their activism: it helped them "become clearer and more thoughtful—more mindful—about their activism" (p. 709); they were better able to integrate a peaceful, nonviolent approach to their work; and they were able to maintain a greater sense of compassion for others. Quieting one's mind is one way to provide space and time for mental rejuvenation.

Some of us may be really good at finding a quiet mind and already use practices regularly to help us. Others of us may have healthy practices at times (when we aren't stressed or distressed), but then when we feel stressed or upset, we may slip into unhealthy practices. Our minds may replay scenarios, prepare for difficult conversations over and over, or just continue to plan and dwell on things that are difficult. The next activity is designed to guide you in experiencing a few minutes of a quieter mind.

## ACTIVITY 7.2

### Clearing Our Mind

There are a number of ways to practice tapping into a quiet mind. There are some approaches supported by research and centuries of tradition yet each individual needs to find what works best for them. Below, we guide you through a basic mindfulness activity. You can choose an alternative activity if you prefer. For example, some people find that prayer, poetry, chanting, or music are good tools to quiet the mind. Find what works for you.

1.  Choose a time and place that will allow you to have 10 to 20 minutes undisturbed (if this is your first time practicing mindful techniques, 5 minutes may be a good start).
2.  Find a comfortable place to sit, perhaps put on music if you choose (without lyrics is best), and find something to gaze at that doesn't require mental energy (a design, a flower or plant, an object, etc.). Set a timer for 5 minutes to start (a gentle bell or ringtone helps continue your state of calm).
3.  Have some water nearby in case you get thirsty.
4.  Breathe slowly (in through your nose, and out through your mouth as though you are blowing through a straw), paying attention to your breath, the rising and lowering of your chest and stomach.
5.  Focus on your breath, the object, or the music. If you find your mind preoccupied or the wheels turning, gently return your attention back to the original focus, your breath. Thich Nhat Hanh, a Vietnamese Buddhist monk and peace activist, suggests thinking about the intruding thoughts as gentle clouds that you observe and let them float away, not fighting them but noticing them and imagining them float on. He also suggests that it is important to be compassionate with ourselves in that process.
6.  When the timer goes off, slowly bring your attention back to the room and your surroundings. Reflect on how that experience was for you, and jot down a few notes. If you found you had some difficulty staying focused, no worries. That often happens, and you will find that it will generally become easier as you continue to practice.

The activity above focuses on body, breath, and attention to help release persistent thoughts. It integrates physical and emotional calm in addition to mental calming. There are a number of other resources and techniques that you might try, depending on your interests. Two great resources we know include the Black Lives Matter Meditation for Racial Healing shared by Candice Crowell, a counseling psychologist (http://drcandicenicole.com/2016/07/black-lives-matter-meditation/), and a wealth of resources and tools for mindfulness and meditation shared by Thich Nhat Hanh and Plum Village (https://plumvillage.org/mindfulness-practice/).

In addition to the distortion that mental fatigue can create in our emotional lives, it can also affect our social or relational well-being. When we are mentally "on" all the time, we may miss out on other lived experiences as well as important relationships with people. When we are so focused on our own issues, we may not let go long enough to listen to what is important to loved ones in our lives. A healthy mind can contribute to healthy relationships.

# The Heart: Our Emotional and Relational Well-Being

We have chosen the metaphor of the heart to represent the importance of emotions in our well-being as well as the role that relationships have in sustaining or draining us. The emotional aspect is the heart focused within and

**FIGURE 7.3** The heart: Our emotional and relational well-being

the relational aspect is our heart extended out toward others. These two aspects of the heart are very interconnected, just as the heart is interconnected with the head, body, and spirit.

## Emotional Well-Being

There is a range of ways that emotional health is viewed, depending on our frame of reference. Physiologically, emotions are our perception of the result of a biochemical process involving neurophysiology (electrical stimulation and neurotransmitters in our brain in response to external or internal stimuli). Some theories of psychology suggest that emotions are a result of our interpretation of life events and the meanings that we give those events or circumstances. Spiritually, emotions may be seen as the expression or experience of our connection or disconnection. Although we each may have our own theory of what emotions are, where they come from, which ones are "acceptable," and how much control we do or "should" have over them, we all experience them. For our discussion, we will consider emotions as the range of feelings we experience—joy, love, happiness, anger, fear, sadness, loneliness, frustration, apathy, and excitement, among others. There are whole books written on emotional health from a wide range of perspectives. We will focus on just two aspects in relation to social action and sustainability: the role of emotions as an alert system and emotions as healthy tools in social action.

When we think about emotions as an alert system, we consider how paying attention to the range of emotions we feel can help us identify what's happening and decide how to proceed in a given situation. For example, when we feel fear or discomfort, that signals us that there might be possible danger. As discussed earlier, it's a good opportunity for us to look at whether the fear or discomfort actually reflects real or imagined danger. Feelings of isolation, loneliness, and disconnection signal that there is something going on in our social and relational life that we may need to attend to. Frustration and anger may signal that there is an injustice happening or something different altogether.

Most of us grow up being taught that certain emotions are more accept-able than others, and we learn patterns of responding. For example, as a girl, I (Rebecca) learned that girls cry when they are sad, angry, frustrated, excited, and lonely; a pretty wide range of emotions. As an adult, I have noticed that I am still learning to accept and use anger in healthy ways. The American Psychological Association provides some useful information to help consider the interaction of our emotions and well-being. For example, "The Road to Resilience" is a resource guide that may be helpful in think-ing about and implementing strategies to help sustain emotional health as well as your physical and relational well-being (https://www.apa.org/helpcenter/road-resilience.aspx).

In addition to the role of emotions as warning signs, emotions can also play an important role in our social action. Scilla Elworthy, in her TED Talk on nonviolence in peace activism, talks about the positive power of anger in emotions (https://www.ted.com/talks/scilla_elworthy_fighting_with_non_violence?language=en). Similarly, research has actually found many positive results of anger (https://www.apa.org/monitor/mar03/whenanger.aspx). If we think about emotions as carrying energy, they can be destructive or constructive. If not channeled or used effectively, anger can end in frustra-tion and a sense of helplessness or harm others. Channeling active emotions such as anger can motivate and energize us, increasing our adrenaline and stamina. When we are fueled by energetic emotions that create adrenaline, we may be more likely to take action and take risks. In this process, we may want to enlist someone that we can check in with to help us make sure that the action we are taking is actually what we intend and support us in using that energy. Fear and anxiety can also be powerful emotions yet can also drain energy or redirect our efforts and make us hesitant to act. In contrast to anger, Elworthy noted that rather than fighting fear and anxiety, it can be helpful to imagine embracing it as we would a child that needs comforting and try to learn what would be helpful to us in that time of fear.

Some classic research looking at surviving and thriving in challenging times can also be helpful. Decades ago, Salvatore Maddi (1987) completed a 12-year study of workers undergoing extreme layoff conditions in their workplace. He found that about two-thirds of the people in his study who faced this stress became depressed and experienced higher levels of physical ailments, whereas another third seemed to sustain and even thrive. Maddi found that those who thrived seemed to hold beliefs that could be described as commitment, control, and challenge attitudes (https://www.apa.org/research/action/lemon.aspx).

The Commitment attitude led them to strive to be involved in ongoing events, rather than feeling isolated. The Control attitude led them to struggle and try to influence outcomes, rather than lapse into passivity and powerlessness. The Challenge attitude led them to view stress changes, whether positive or negative, as opportunities for new learning.

Although we know that everyone has different circumstances and con-texts—there are very real power differences in societies and communities—the three themes above can be helpful in thinking about how we relate to challenging circumstances and social action. There are some similarities between these three themes and the findings of research about peace activists and sustainability. Revisiting Downton and Wehr's (1998) study, we learn that peace activists were likely to have created close relationships with other peace activists and with leaders, although to a lesser extent. The activists described the importance of mutual respect, shared experiences, caring for each other, and sharing feelings of hope. Similarly, DeRay McKesson, activist and former middle school teacher, described the importance of relationships in his activist experiences in Ferguson, Missouri, after the killing of Michael Brown.

> In the beginning, we didn't know each other's names but we knew each other's hearts. There were people that I trusted my life with that I've never seen again, I don't know anything about them. But we hopped the three fences, to get to the whatever ... it was the beginning of a new community. (McKesson, *Combat Jack* podcast)

This sentiment leads us to the second aspect of the heart: our connections with others.

## Relational Well-Being

Relationships sustain us emotionally and socially as well as support our emotional well-being and help us to feel connected and accompanied. Positive social interaction feeds human well-being and cares for us emotionally and spiritually. The warmth of shared values and beliefs helps us to feel a sense of belonging, and the diversity of opinions that come from relating with others can help us to see issues from different perspectives.

One of the challenges that can arise in relationships is a sense of isolation when we feel like we are alone in our beliefs or that the people we care about don't share the same values as we do. Not everyone needs to agree with us, and a diversity of viewpoints makes for richer and broader opportunities for expanding our understanding of the world. The challenge comes when we have very few people who share our perspective or when people we spend a lot of time with have such different viewpoints about things that are very important to us. One of the striking things that has been increasingly reported over the past couple of years is the disruption in personal relationships due to political differences. Conflicts within families, workplaces, and friendships that arise because of differing political viewpoints have resulted in fractures in relationships. This has also given rise to a search for ways to bridge these challenging divides. We don't need to agree with all of the people we care about, yet when we talk about sustainability, it is important to have a solid base of at least some people who share our worldview and feel passionate about the issues we care about.

The following activity is designed to help you explore with whom you share values and issues you care about. Following the activity, we will talk a little about possible strategies you could consider if you find conflicts between your values and those of others.

## ACTIVITY 7.3

### Where Do You Stand, and Who Stands with You?

1. Before you start this activity, take a look at the values you identified in the Values exercises in Chapter 2 (especially Activities 2.4 and 2.5).
2. Then, in the table below, list eight of the values or issues you chose as most important to you in the first column.
3. For each value, think about the people around you and whether they hold and demonstrate the same value. Think about each of the following groups: **You; Your Family; Your Community; Your Coworkers; and Society.** List each group in the boxes according to how much they share that value. For example, if one of my values is harmony, I think about my family, my community (however I define that), my coworkers, and society, and decide whether and how much they value harmony. If I think my family values it somewhat, my community somewhat, coworkers somewhat, and society only a little, then I write that in the boxes below (see example).

| Example Value | Does Not Value | Values A Little | Somewhat Values | Highly Values |
|---|---|---|---|---|
| Harmony | | Society | My community, my family, my coworkers | Me |

Now, think about the people and communities in your life. Where do they fall on your Values continuum? Write in each group (You; Your

Family; Your Community; Your Coworkers; and Society) based on the extent to which they value each of the values you have listed below.

**Your Values:**

| Top 8 Values | Does Not Value | Values a Little | Somewhat Values | Highly Values |
|---|---|---|---|---|
| 1. | | | | |
| 2. | | | | |
| 3. | | | | |
| 4. | | | | |
| 5. | | | | |
| 6. | | | | |
| 7. | | | | |
| 8. | | | | |

Now that you have placed everyone on the Values table, take a look at who seems to hold similar values and who seems to be different from you. Are there values where you feel most alone? Are there values that are shared by many?

In reflecting on this activity, if you find that you have company—in other words, your family, community, coworkers, and society seem to value the same things you do—then you may feel less of a need to explain your motivations for your actions. In this case, you may feel like you have people you can vent to, brainstorm with, or simply spend time with enjoyably. If you find that there are strong differences and very few people who share that value, then you may want to think about some steps to care for yourself and manage those relationships in a way that doesn't feel too costly or stressful. That may be helpful to recognize differences in values and adjust what we expect from those relationships. For sustaining our emotional health in the process, it is important to also have other friends, family members, and community members with whom we feel a shared sense of values and can provide support.

For many of us, finding solidarity with others who care about similar issues is a major act of self-care and sustainability. In this way, participating in demonstrations and social forms of action may help break feelings of isolation and being overwhelmed. Sometimes, we must separate out the relationships that we have and consider that not every relationship will fulfill all of our needs. However, it is reasonable to expect to have at least some relationships where we feel respected and supported for our values and how we act on those. It also helps to feel a sense of camaraderie when others share our values and commitment to act. For people who engage in activism, it is often helpful to have connections with others who can relate to that experience, for example, engaging in support and self-help groups. In an interview on self-care for activists, Bree Mae, an activist, describes the importance for her of finding an activism support group to reflect and recharge regularly (https://www.youtube.com/watch?v=nfzMqqqi9ko). Support groups, activism resource centers, online interest groups, and chat groups can all provide that sense of camaraderie. The Interhelp Network is one resource that provides guidance on developing and engaging in support groups specifically oriented for folks engaged in social change (https://interhelpnetwork.org/keeping-us-going-a-manual-on-support-groups-for-social-change-activists/). It is also important to develop the skills to recognize when these groups may not be helpful and how to disengage if we find them toxic and unhealthy.

There is a lot we can do to maintain balance, care for ourselves, repair hurt, and invest in healthy relationships. It can also be very helpful to consider reaching out for help from those who are trained and have expertise. The American Psychological Association provides information about psychotherapy that can be helpful for those who are unfamiliar with this way of receiving support (https://www.apa.org/helpcenter/psychotherapy-works.aspx). Depending on your economic resources (including health insurance) and where you live or work, you may even have access to mental health professionals who specialize in providing support for activists and community organizers.

## The Body: Our Physical Well-Being

Sustainability in terms of physical health is both obvious and elusive. We will address two aspects: caring for our physical self and being compassionate with our physical self. These are related but slightly separate, with the first referring to actions we can take to maintain healthy physical functioning and the second referring to the acknowledgment that sometimes our physical self requires that we step away, pull back, or rest for a little while.

**FIGURE 7.4**  The body: Our physical well-being

## Caring for Our Physical Self

Advice on physical health and exercise is everywhere in the United States today, and yet, we often find it difficult to do the things we know are good for us: paying attention to what we eat and drink, getting exercise, regular and sufficient sleep, and being careful about things we ingest that have negative effects on our physical health and stamina (e.g., caffeine, nicotine, sugar, etc.). There are certainly differences in how easily different communities can access ingredients for basic healthy lifestyles, as we can see challenges to health presented by unsafe neighborhoods limiting out-door activity, lack of clean water, lack of affordable healthy food, necessity of multiple jobs to afford housing, and other barriers. For some of us, these barriers may be a target for our activism. In other words, the social action issues we focus on hopefully help create more equitable access to these basic building blocks for health. For others of us, it is not these real barriers that limit us, but rather our own choices that lead us toward less healthy ways of living. This is even more prominent when we are feeling stressed or overcommitted. It's often a vicious circle in that we get stressed and feel like we have too much to do so we keep working, we get less sleep, we don't exercise, and our meals become irregular and less healthy. All of this results in us becoming even less healthy and we feel even less energetic and able to do the things we feel like we need to do. For those of us who have chronic illnesses, vulnerable health, and physical challenges, there may be added complexities to what is needed to maintain our health. In this section devoted to physical health, we are assuming that each of our individual situations is different with a range of resources available to us for physical health. Further, we assume that we all have a range of experiences with physical health challenges. Still, within our unique situation we can look at the options we have, the choices we make, and the possibilities we have not yet considered.

The recommendations for maintaining our physical health are probably not surprising to anyone reading this. Sometimes additional evidence can help propel us to healthier behaviors, at least temporarily (e.g., research on the addictive properties of sugar and the prevalence of sugar in most processed foods, the health benefits of at least 30 minutes of exercise per day, the negative impact of sleep deprivation on mental health, physical health and aging, etc.). Even with evidence, we often struggle to maintain healthy patterns. The challenges to maintaining physical health are both at an individual level (i.e., what we control in our own lives) and systemic (i.e., how our environment and society support or interfere in healthy living).

Starting with the individual level and using a strength-based framework, let's consider when we seem to best be able to take care of our physical self and then build on that.

---

### ACTIVITY 7.4

### Good Times and Challenging Times

This activity is focused on increasing how well you take care of your physical health. Sometimes when we become stressed at work, everything seems urgent. Thus, we may work longer hours and, even when we're not working, may be preoccupied with work. It doesn't feel like we have ANY time to take a break, not even 30 minutes to take a walk. This activity guides you in finding out what works for you to best take care of yourself, what interferes, and what small changes you can make to integrate care more consistently.

1. **The Good Times:** Think about a recent time when you had at least one week of taking good care of your physical self. Try to recall some details:
   a. How were you "taking good care" of your physical self? (e.g., eating, exercise, sleeping)
   b. What was happening in your life during that time? (e.g., where were you? Who were you with? What demands were placed on you?)

    c.   What made it easier to take care of your physical self? (e.g., routine, buddy, etc.)

2. **The Challenging Times:** Now, think about a time in the recent past when you were not taking good care of your physical self for at least a week. Try to recall some details:

    a.   How were you "<u>not</u> taking good care" of your physical self? (e.g., eating, exercise, sleeping)

    b.   What was happening in your life during that time? (e.g., where were you? Who were you with? What demands were placed on you?)

    c.   What made it harder to take care of your physical self? (e.g., no routine, too busy, etc.)

3. What were some of the differences between the good times and the challenging times?

4. Now, think about three small things you can put in an imaginary emergency box to pull out during those challenging times. For example, 15 minutes to stretch, drink an extra glass of water, etc. Write those three things in the chart below.

5. Over a week, track the three things you did each day. Each day, write down how difficult it was to do those three things, and what you noticed when you were doing it and after you did it.

6. On the last row, write three words each evening to describe how you feel.

|  | Sun | Mon | Tues | Wed | Thurs | Fri | Sat |
|---|---|---|---|---|---|---|---|
| Thing 1: |  |  |  |  |  |  |  |
| Thing 2: |  |  |  |  |  |  |  |
| Thing 3: |  |  |  |  |  |  |  |
| Reflections at night: Three words to describe how you feel |  |  |  |  |  |  |  |

As you reflect on the week, how difficult was it to consistently do the three things you identified? What made it difficult or easy? If it was very difficult, consider three other things that might be easier to introduce during stressful times and try again, or, consider what might need to be adjusted in your life to make room for healthy practices.

This activity is just a start, and a week of something new is really not enough time to draw conclusions. However, it may give you the opportunity to get started and see some small successes. It is important to note that for many of us, we might start off intending to follow through, but then something comes up, or we forget, or just don't do it. If that's the case, try again, with no blame and no judgment. Consider what interfered with you doing three things. Sometimes it's that we start too big or just haven't shifted our patterns. If you can, try it for three weeks and see what a new habit may feel like.

## Compassion for Our Physical Self

In addition to maintaining our physical health and well-being, we also need to acknowledge that sometimes we may be physically at our limit. The Sustainability section of the S-quad model is intended to remind us that it's okay to step back, whether because we have other demands in our life or because our health needs attention. In her contribution to *The Impossible Will Take a Little While* (2004), Danusha Veronica Goska shared the following insights regarding the challenges of her physical condition and her connection to social action.

> On some days I was functional. On others, and I could never predict when those days would strike, I was literally, not metaphorically, paralyzed ... that paralysis has taught me something. It has taught me that my protestations of my own powerlessness are bogus. Yes, some days I can't move or see. And the difference between being able to walk across the room and not being able to walk across the room is epic ... The problem is not that we have so little power. The problem is that we don't use the power that we have. (Goska, pp. 47–48)

In your life, consider the self-compassion that might be helpful in sustaining your efforts in the long term. If you worry that self-care or stepping back from action is avoidance from social action, begin noting on your calendar when to check back in on yourself. Although we can't always predict when our physical challenges will be stabilized enough to get back into action, sometimes it can be helpful to know that we have a designated time to regroup.

# The Spirit: Our Essence, or Our Connection to Something Greater than Ourselves

Nourishing your heart can involve giving and receiving love; taking care of one's mind may relate to mental stimulation, growth, and quiet; taking care of one's body can include physical exercise and rest; and spirituality may mean paying attention to your soul and taking care of your spirit. The *spirit* represents our sense of connection to something greater than ourselves, whether it be our principles, values, belief in a

**FIGURE 7.5** The Spirit: Our essence or our connection to something greater than ourselves

higher power or a greater being, connection to a shared history, or other aspects. This is different for everyone, and we all have varying degrees to which this is present consciously in our lives. We (Rebecca and Muninder) acknowledge that for some people, the spirit is the core of their lives, while for others, spirituality is not an area of importance or belief.

Spirituality can be a belief in the teachings of a shared religious or spiritual practice. Cultural traditions and beliefs can shape, support, and connect us to a spiritual life such as through meditation, prayer, and song. Alternatively, spirituality may not be related to an organized system or community but may be more of a reflection of beliefs about the nature of life, the universe, human- and animal-kind, our connection to living beings and nature, or in other ways that we are deeply rooted. Even for those of us who don't identify with a greater being, religious practice, or spirituality per se, we may have some connection to a sense of meaning and a purpose. It is that sense that we refer to as spirit.

---

**EXAMPLE**

### Muninder's Reflections on Spirituality

For me, spirituality is in the context of religion and means being connected to something bigger than myself, in particular with my community, with humanity, and to God. I become in tune or in flow with something meaningful outside myself, but I also pay attention to how it resonates within myself. I can engage in religious practice on my own, but being in gurdwara allows me to be immersed in the Sikh community, pray with others, sing *shabads* (hymns) in unison, engage in seva, hear the lessons of our ten Gurus, be in the presence of the *Guru Granth Sahib* (the Sikh holy book), and share a meal prepared by the congregation for all who wish to partake. For Sikhs, religion allows us a venue by which to ask for guidance and support, celebrate joyous occasions by expressing gratitude, receive and provide solace in times of distress, and promote social justice.

### EXAMPLE

### Rebecca's Reflections on Spirituality

I think about spirituality as the core of my being that is connected to the outer world through music, creativity, intimacy, shared experiences, connection with nature, and art. Although I was raised Catholic, and some of my beliefs about justice and community come from some of the teachings, I do not hold many of the beliefs that are still present in the Catholic religion and my conception of spirituality and higher powers is different than what is often taught in Catholicism. My adult spirituality is not connected to a religious community or specific practice but is related to my everyday practices and beliefs.

There is a belief in Sikhism, and in many religions, that if you are not in the community of people who are like yourself, you can become spiritually bereft. I (Muninder) take a view of this that goes beyond religion and includes other shared identities. For racial, ethnic, and religious minorities, nourishing the spirit involves being with people who look like you and people who share your values and beliefs, particularly if you live and work in places where you don't regularly see people like yourself. It allows a coming together for People of Color and of minority faiths to fight against "-isms" (e.g., racism, anti-Semitism, Islamophobia). For many immigrants, religion and spirituality can offer a consistent sense of home, a naturally existing community to connect with after moving to a new country, and a place to hear one's language spoken as a means of connection.

Though religion is a powerful tool that nourishes and develops my (Muninder's) spirit, I also know that for some people, religion is the antithesis of spirituality. It can be even more complicated for many people because both positive spirituality and oppression coexist in religion. Religious systems have been used to oppress different groups of people over time (e.g., women, LGBTQ individuals), and religion has been used as a politically divisive tool. When understanding how your spirit may or may not be connected to religion, it is important to pay attention to ways in which religion or spirituality have been used to promote and/or block social justice for you, for your community, and for others.

### Visualizing Your Spiritual Well-Being—A Collage

The purpose of this collage is to create a representation of what you consider to be a part of your spiritual well-being and to reflect on whether you allow yourself the time and space to include attention to this in your daily life. *(If you feel that spirituality is not at all a part of your experience and you prefer to skip this activity, feel free to do so.)*

Get a large piece of paper, a board, or use digital tools on the computer. Select words, quotes, images, songs, and photos that help you define your spirit and what nourishes your spiritual well-being.

1. What do the representations (words, pictures, images) mean to you?
2. How do you feel when you are looking at this board?
3. Is there something missing that you would like to add in the future?
4. What activities do you currently engage in that develop and support the well-being of your spirit (e.g., spiritual or religious)? What activities could you add?
   a.
   b.
5. How do these things help to bring balance and well-being to your life?
6. Are there things that you are not doing that would help you to feel more balanced, at peace, and/or fulfilled spiritually? How might you build those into your life?

If, upon reflecting on your spiritual health, you find that there are practices that you find useful but you seem to neglect in your life, it may be helpful to spend a little time considering how to address that. For example, you might consider using the physical health activity (Activity 7.4) and adapt it to reflect spiritual practices. In this way, you can reflect on a time when you felt balanced and healthy spiritually and when you did not. Consider the conditions and practices that helped you to maintain that sense of balance.

Now that we have taken a journey through different aspects of wellness and personal sustainability, diving into the individual elements, we want to come back to a sense of wholeness. Personal sustainability is best when it acknowledges and attends to the bigger picture of our well-being. The next section guides you through developing a plan to help you do just that.

# Your Big Picture of Sustainability

There is no one right way to work toward health and wellness in the face of challenge. In this section, we will guide you through an activity to reflect on your own experience, personality, and spirit to help you create a sustainability plan, including resources and strategies that you might find helpful depending on your life, work, style, and spirit of wellness.

## ACTIVITY 7.6

### Sustainability Menu

**Part 1:** In the table below, list as many sustainability activities you can think of that you might feasibly engage in. Reflect back on the activities you have done so far to identify activities that provide you with positive energy, joy, connection, rest, peace, balance, and other healthy conditions. For each one, include symbols to indicate what might be required in order to engage in that activity. Then put an **X** to indicate which aspect of your well-being might be nurtured by that activity.

Symbols:
  $- requires money
  T- requires a fair amount of time
  P- requires the cooperation of others
  A- requires advanced planning

| Activity | Mind | Heart: Emotions | Heart: Relational | Body | Spirit |
|---|---|---|---|---|---|
| (Example) go dancing with friends ($, T, P, A) | x | x | x | x | x |
| Go to beach | T X | X | | | |
| read bible | X | X | X | X | X |
| nap | | | | X | |
| swim | T | | | X | |
| dinner friends $AXP | | | X | | |
| read book | X | X | | | X |
| surf | T | | | X | |
| paint nails | X | | | | |
| watch sunset | X | | | | |

**Part 2:** Choose two of these activities that you can schedule weekly so they become a part of your regular routine.
Reading my bible & swimming

**Part 3:** Create two surprise boxes.

- On an index card, write each of the activities that you thought of (from the table in Part 1).
- Separate the cards into two piles: one that requires little time, money, or planning, and the other pile contains cards that require more time, money, or planning.
- Each pile will have its own box: "easy" and "extended" (you can make up your own names).
- If you'd like, you can decorate each box with photos or pictures that represent the kinds of activities in the box.

**Part 4:** At least once a week, choose two cards from the "easy" box and do them. Decide how often to choose a card from the "extended" box and plan when you might do it.

As a final note about your sustainability plan, we would like to advocate for the idea of a "sustainability buddy." This is someone who helps to let you know when you seem to be slipping away from healthy practices, who can join you in joyful activities, and who can sit with you when you're feeling sad. Of course, this buddy relationship works both ways: to have a buddy, you need to be a buddy too. For us (Rebecca and Muninder), we have been sustainability buddies for each other for over 17 years and have supported each other through difficult times and even every day hiccups. In fact, for us, having each other as sustainability buddies has been a wellness strategy in and of itself.

## Additional Sustainability Resources

As noted throughout this workbook, our experiences and identities influence our work and the way others respond to us. When we are working toward justice in areas that affect us and/or our community, we feel the toll that it takes even more personally. We may be retriggered, we may be targeted, and we may feel the pain of others. There is wisdom that is shared by leaders, artists, and others who have felt trauma and persisted. A beautiful resource for people who have experienced racial trauma is *Healing in Action* from Black Lives Matter (https://blacklivesmatter.com/wp-content/uploads/2017/10/BLM_HealinginAction-1-1.pdf). This guide integrates awareness about the unique costs experienced by folks who have racial trauma when they engage in activism, especially given the intensity and frequency of anti-black, anti-LGBT, anti-immigrant, and anti–People of Color rhetoric and opposition they may face.

In addition to some of the strategies we describe here, there is a growing number of resources for wellness. One in development by psychologists Isaac Prilleltensky and his colleagues is "Fun for Wellness," a comprehensive online wellness assessment and activities tool (https://www.funforwellness.com/fun/index.html) designed to reduce stress and increase feelings of wellness. Another resource is Esther Brownsmith's online op-ed that provides great links to a range of useful websites and tools for self-care (https://indivisiblesomerville.org/new-to-activism-grow-your-practices-of-self-care/).

The resources above tend to focus on helping us care for ourselves at an individual or personal level. Michael Leiter and Christine Maslach, two researchers who have extensively studied burnout in many occupations, suggest that preventing burnout in activism needs to be done at a personal and institutional level (2005). In other words, it is important that we cope and prevent burnout in the ways that we engage in activism and social action as well as to look at the approaches of social change organizations and larger efforts. If we think about an automobile as a metaphor for a movement or social change organization, we can consider that it needs fuel and there are many moving parts that depend on each other. Maintenance is required to keep each part functioning, and it is also necessary for them to function well together. Lubrication, cleaning, and preventing wear and tear all need attention. Sometimes we need to retire parts when they become worn out, otherwise they can potentially damage other parts or the whole system itself. Some of the elements discussed in the earlier Strategies section, especially regarding working with groups, can be helpful in thinking about the dynamics that can arise when working with groups. Adrienne Maree Brown, in *Emergent Strategy* (2017), talks about understanding our role within social movements and how we can contribute in ways that support movements as well as what to do when we feel critical. The Community Toolbox (https://ctb.ku.edu/en/table-of-contents/assessment/promotion-strategies/maintain-a-coalition/main) also describes very user-friendly strategies for maintaining coalitions.

Creating a routine for everyday action can help with sustainability in that it can help you make social action a part of your life, rather than an add-on. When we are exhausted or burnt out, we may be ineffective—or worse, harmful to others or to the cause we care about. When we integrate sustainability practices, we cannot only keep moving forward in a positive direction, but also help others do the same. Many of the strategies you have identified here can be built into your routine alongside sustainability activities you already engage in. Set goals for what is realistic for you. Finally, we would like to suggest that many of the activities and reflections you did earlier in the book can be helpful now. Take a look at what you wrote in the beginning of this workbook about your heroes, lessons learned, and your vision. These can all help you refocus and reenergize when you get discouraged. These can be your guiding forces to help you stay on a healthful path.

# section 3

**Bringing It All Together**

# chapter eight

# Moving Forward from Here

## Closing

As we near the end of this workbook, we would like to reflect back on our journey together. The intent of this workbook is to be a catalyst, a motivating force, and an organizing tool, to help readers thoughtfully and intentionally take action around issues they care about. The four areas of reflection—Strength, Solidarity, Strategy, and Sustainability—present opportunities and challenges for each of us. Through the information and activities that we presented to you, you have engaged in self-reflection and taken action. This is a continual and evolving process. Each new situation presents different circumstances: your strengths and assets will grow and change; communities and your relationships will shift and change; the approach that is needed in one situation may be totally different in another; and your life and your capacity to engage in social action will evolve and sometimes fluctuate. Mindfully and intentionally engaging in reflection, skill building, relationship building, and action will be essential.

In the beginning (Chapter 2), we explored the issues you care about and the importance of being able to focus your efforts. Reflecting on your stories, your beliefs and values, and the issues happening in the world and community, we asked you to choose a focus for the work you would do in this book. Having focused on an issue, we then embarked on a process of reflection and action and introduced each of the four areas of reflection (Chapter 3). We would like to revisit those here and encourage you to make notes about your insights and your future directions.

## Strengths, Assets, and Resources

In this area of reflection (Chapter 4), you took stock of the strengths, skills, and knowledge you already possess personally and through your work and training. Assets and resources also include your ability to find and access things that can be helpful in social action given your connection to people or places that hold those resources. In addition, you looked at how your life experience and the identities you hold also contribute to the strengths you bring to social action. Further, understanding your own identities and your connection to the issues you care about makes a difference in terms of solidarity and strategy.

Gathering the strengths, assets, and resources you already have is the first area of reflection because it is the foundation—what you already have and can bring to the table right now. We emphasized that you have expertise and can use that as you take action now. You also spent some time identifying areas where you might grow, additional strengths, and potential resources.

## Solidarity

Knowing the strengths and resources you have as well as how you relate to the issues you care about, you then turned to the second area of reflection: Solidarity (Chapter 5). In this chapter, we emphasized the importance of building relationships and the many benefits of maintaining them, including honoring relationships and sustaining community; respecting, supporting, and understanding others; finding strength in numbers; and seeking support and camaraderie to help sustain you. We talked about the importance of understanding who you are in relation to the issues you are addressing and how relationships with people who have a range of experience and strengths can make action more relevant and effective. We also reflected on how powerful it can be when we are connected with others.

## Strategy

Taking action in a thoughtful and planful way requires strategy, the third area of reflection. In Chapter 6, we reviewed a multitude of different approaches to taking action as well as some guidance in choosing the form of action that may fit the situation and issue you are addressing. Having a big picture view of what change is needed and then using a "playbook," or specific types of action, can help you systematically and strategically contribute to work that is already happening or to get something started yourself. The form of action you take could be contacting legislators and policy makers, entering politics yourself, reaching out to media or creating media, participating or initiating public demonstrations through rallies, art, music, and many other options. We acknowledge that sometimes there are consequences to our actions, especially because we are often going against large and powerful systems. We also recognize that the repercussions may be harsher for some people than others given individual and systemic discrimination and oppression. Thus, choosing a strategy may also involve understanding your positionality and your identities and how they relate to those in power.

We also discussed strategies for what we call "everyday action." These are things you can do daily without a lot of preparation. For example, making a commitment to stand up to oppression, having legislators on speed dial, and other actions can all contribute to change. Social change requires all kinds of action. Different levels, longer term strategies, and everyday action help continue forward movement and help you to know that you are doing something to make things better.

## Sustainability

For many of us the costs to justice and human rights, the harm that is being done to families, the rights that are ignored daily for many people, the damage of poverty, and so many other injustices present necessary targets for social change. Yet, they can sometimes feel overwhelming. Sustainability is the process of attending to yourself, your family, and your life on a regular basis throughout social action to help you maintain stamina, balance, and vitality. Our well-being is a multidimensional picture that includes our physical, mental, emotional/relational, and spiritual health. Without our well-being, it is very hard for us to be effective change agents over the long run.

## Moving Forward

We hope this workbook helped you engage in a process to move forward in your efforts to act for social change. We expect that you may have already known much of what is in the workbook, yet we hope that it spurred you to think of areas you may have neglected or simply encouraged you to persist, even when it feels difficult. We were very aware as we wrote this book that we were not able to include everything that could be helpful. Further, as we come to the end of the workbook, we want to emphasize that this is by no means coming to the end of the process. The four areas of reflection, strength, solidarity, strategy and sustainability, are cyclical, as represented by the graphic of the four Ss. They are interwoven together, and each is revisited at various times, depending on the challenges you are encountering or the different circumstances your life presents.

We want to end this book by reflecting back on our process of writing and your process of reading the book. You may have felt a variety of emotions as you went through each portion of the four Ss. We know we did in writing it. Emotions, if read right, can be helpful to us in each of the four Ss—they are signals. For us, the book was important to help us move from a place of hopelessness to a rekindling of hope, strategically moving us into action with others, and sustaining ourselves, others, and our justice work. We hope this book helps you to do the work that is so important to you and to share these ideas and steps with others. You may have found tools to engage in social justice action in ways that refined what you already do or in new ways. Through this book and beyond, we walk alongside you as you try to maintain that spirit of *Chardi Kala*—eternal optimism in the face of oppression—and find ways of working that will allow you to continue to fight the good fight.

# References

Alicia, J., Bergman, M., Boone, E., Cervantes, S.K., Desai, M., Littleton, Y. & Pérez, I. (2019). *Maestrapeace: San Francisco's monumental feminist mural.* Berkeley, CA: Heyday Books.

Brown, A. M. (2017). *Emergent strategy: Shaping change, changing worlds.* Chico, CA: AK Press.

DeBlaere, C., Brewster, M. E., Bertsch, K. N., DeCarlo, A. L., Kegel, K. A., & Presseau, C. D. (2014). The protective power of collective action for sexual minority women of color: An investigation of multiple discrimination experiences and psychological distress. *Psychology of Women Quarterly, 38*(1), 20–32.

Downton, J., & Wehr, P. (1998). Persistent pacifism: How activist commitment is developed and sustained. *Journal of Peace Research, 35*(5), 531–550. doi:https://doi.org/10.1177/0022343398035005001

Flaherty, J. (2016). *No more heroes: Grassroots challenges to the savior mentality.* Chico, CA: AK Press.

Freudenberger, H. J., & Richelson, G. (1980). *Burn-out: The high cost of high achievement.* Anchor Press ed. Garden City, NY: Anchor Press.

Gorski, P. C. (2015). Relieving burnout and the "martyr syndrome" among social justice education activists: The implications and effects of mindfulness. *Urban Review, 47*(4), 696–716. https://doi.org.jpllnet.sfsu.edu/10.1007/s11256-015-0330-0

Goska, D. V. (2004). Political paralysis. In P. R. Loeb (Ed.), *The impossible will take a little while: A citizen's guide to hope in a time of fear* (pp. 47–62). New York, NY: Basic Books.

Hays, P. A. (1996). Addressing the complexities of culture and gender in counseling. *Journal of Counseling & Development, 74*, 332–338.

Hays, P. A. (2008). *Addressing cultural complexities in practice: Assessment, diagnosis, and therapy* (2nd ed.). Washington, DC: American Psychological Association.

Leiter, M. P., & Maslach, C. (2005). *Banishing burnout: Six strategies for improving your relationship with work.* San Francisco, CA: Jossey-Bass.

Kristofferson, K., White, K., & Peloza, J. (2014). The nature of slacktivism: How the social observability of an initial act of token support affects subsequent prosocial action. *Journal of Consumer Research, 40*(6), 1149–1166. doi:10.1086/674137

Kovan, J. T., & Dirkx, J. M. (2003). "Being called awake": The role of transformative learning in the lives of environmental activists. *Adult Education Quarterly, 53*(2), 99–118. https://doi.org.jpllnet.sfsu.edu/10.1177/0741713602238906

Maddi, S. R. (1987). Hardiness training at Illinois Bell Telephone. In J. P. Opatz (Ed.), *Health promotion evaluation* (pp. 101–115). Stevens Point, WI: National Wellness Institute.

McDonnell, M.-H., & Werner, T. (2016). Blacklisted businesses: Social activists' challenges and the disruption of corporate political activity. *Administrative Science Quarterly, 61*(4), 584–620. https://doi.org/10.1177/0001839216648953

Odağ, O., Uluğ, O. M., & Solak, N. (2016). "Everyday I'm Çapuling": Identity and collective action through social network sites in the Gezi Park protests in Turkey. *Journal of Media Psychology, 28*, 148–159. Retrieved from https://doi.org/10.1027/1864-1105/a000202

Orangias, J., Simms, J., & French, S. (2017). The cultural functions and social potential of queer monuments: A preliminary inventory and analysis. *Journal of Homosexuality, 65*(6), 705–726. doi:10.1080/00918369.2017.1364106

Pierce, C., Carew, J., Pierce-Gonzalez, D., & Willis, D. (1978). An experiment in racism: TV commercials. In C. Pierce (Ed.), *Television and education* (pp. 62–88). Beverly Hills, CA: Sage.

Prado, D. (2017, May 9). "Woke Twitter" can be problematic: A movement solely reliant on likes and social shares will not stand a chance. HuffPost. Retrieved from https://www.huffpost.com/entry/how-woke-twitter-can-be-problematic_b_5910c559e4b0f71180724740

Roediger, D. R. (2018). *Working toward whiteness: How America's immigrants became white: The strange journey from Ellis Island to the suburbs.* New York, NY: Basic Books.

Sue, D. W. (2010). *Microaggressions in everyday life: Race, gender, and sexual orientation.* Hoboken, NJ: Wiley & Sons.

Sue, D. W., Alsaidi, S., Awad, M. N., Glaeser, E., Calle, C. Z., & Mendez, N. (2019). Disarming racial microaggressions: Microintervention strategies for targets, White allies, and bystanders. *American Psychologist, 74*(1), 128–142. http://dx.doi.org/10.1037/amp0000296

Sue, D. W., Capodilupo, C. M., Torino, G. C., Bucceri, J. M., Holder, A. M. B., Nadal, K. L., & Esquilin, M. (2007). Racial microaggressions in everyday life: Implications for clinical practice. *American Psychologist, 62*(4), 271–286. http://dx.doi.org/10.1037/0003-066X.62.4.271

Szymanski, D. M., & Owens, G. P. (2009). Group-level coping as a moderator between heterosexism and sexism and psychological distress in sexual minority women. *Psychology of Women Quarterly, 33*(2), 197–205. https://doi.org/10.1111/j.1471-6402.2009.01489.x

Uhl-Bien, M., Riggio, R. E., Lowe, K. B., & Carsten, M. K. (2014). Followership theory: A review and research agenda. *Leadership Quarterly, 25*(1), 83–104. https://doi-org.jpllnet.sfsu.edu/10.1016/j.leaqua.2013.11.007